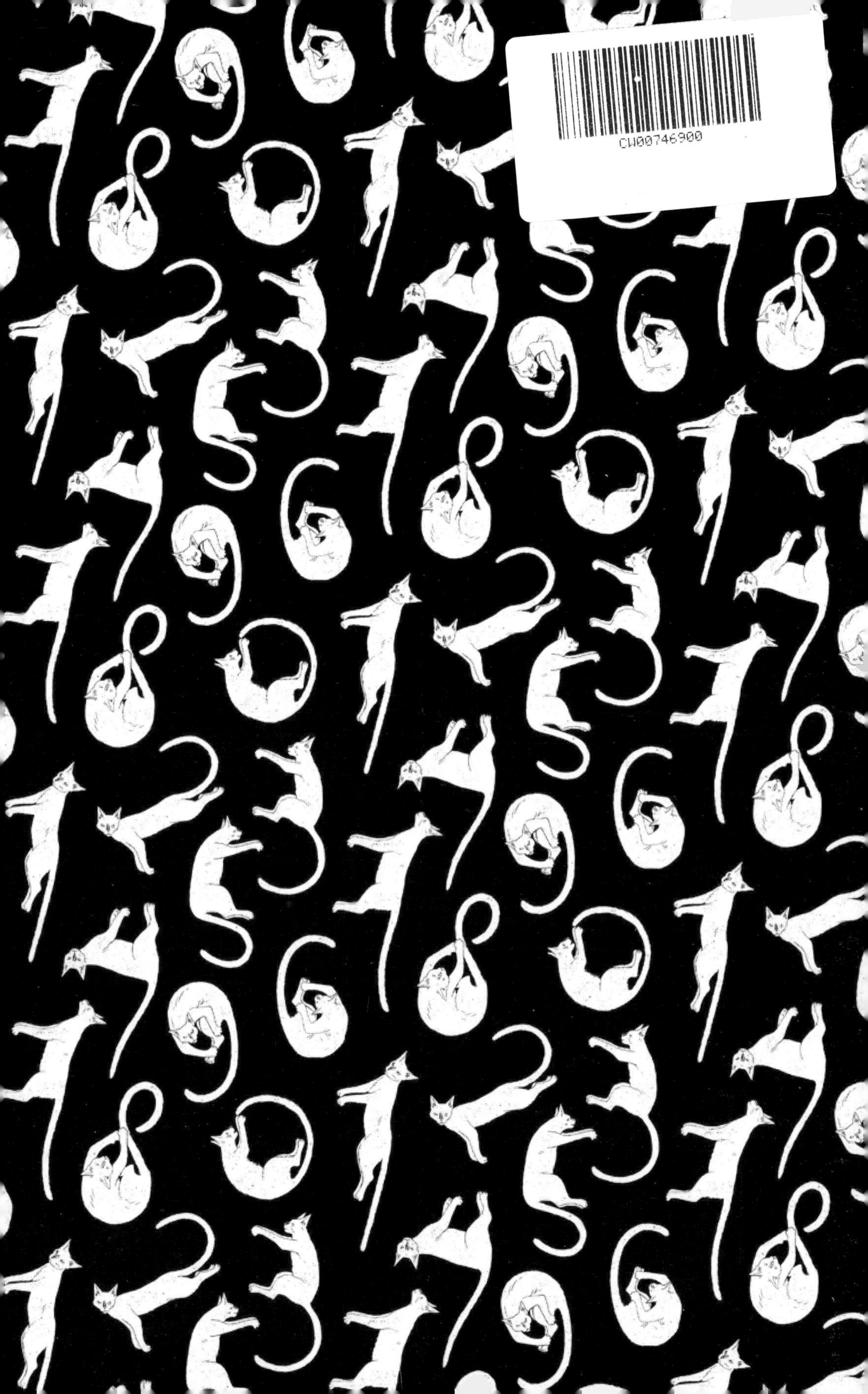

Serge Baeken

translated by
Michele
Hutchison

SUGAR

Life as a
Cat

Soaring Penguin Press

SUGAR

Life as a Cat

By Serge Baeken

Translated by Michele Hutchison

Published by Soaring Penguin Press
4 Florence Terrace
London
SW15 3RU
www.soaringpenguinpress.com

ISBN 978-1-908030-28-3

Printed in Ukraine.

This book was published with the support of Flanders Literature (flandersliterature.be).

This album is dedicated to all my cats:
Tim, Jeffie, Franciscus (Sugar), Ghiselda, Igor, Maya, Pogo and Ricky.
Many thanks to Annsje, Carmen, Eva, Ria, Kim and Kathleen.

Sugar is finished at last. At last: after years of diligently working on different storylines, my dear friend Serge Baeken opted for an innovative and experimental approach. He used a robust layout for the frames with constantly changing perspectives to show the world through the eyes of a cat. And not just any cat. A cat called Sugar. The anecdotes are recognizable, tender, melancholic, sad. But actually it's rather a shame that the album has been finished. Who is going to send me graceful drawings each week, surprise me with virtuoso sketches and make me laugh or cry at the mischievous adventures of – dammit– his four-legged friends? Perhaps I should be secretly hoping for a brilliant sequel. Sugar 2 – sounds good, doesn't it. *

Ephameron

*From the original Flemish edition

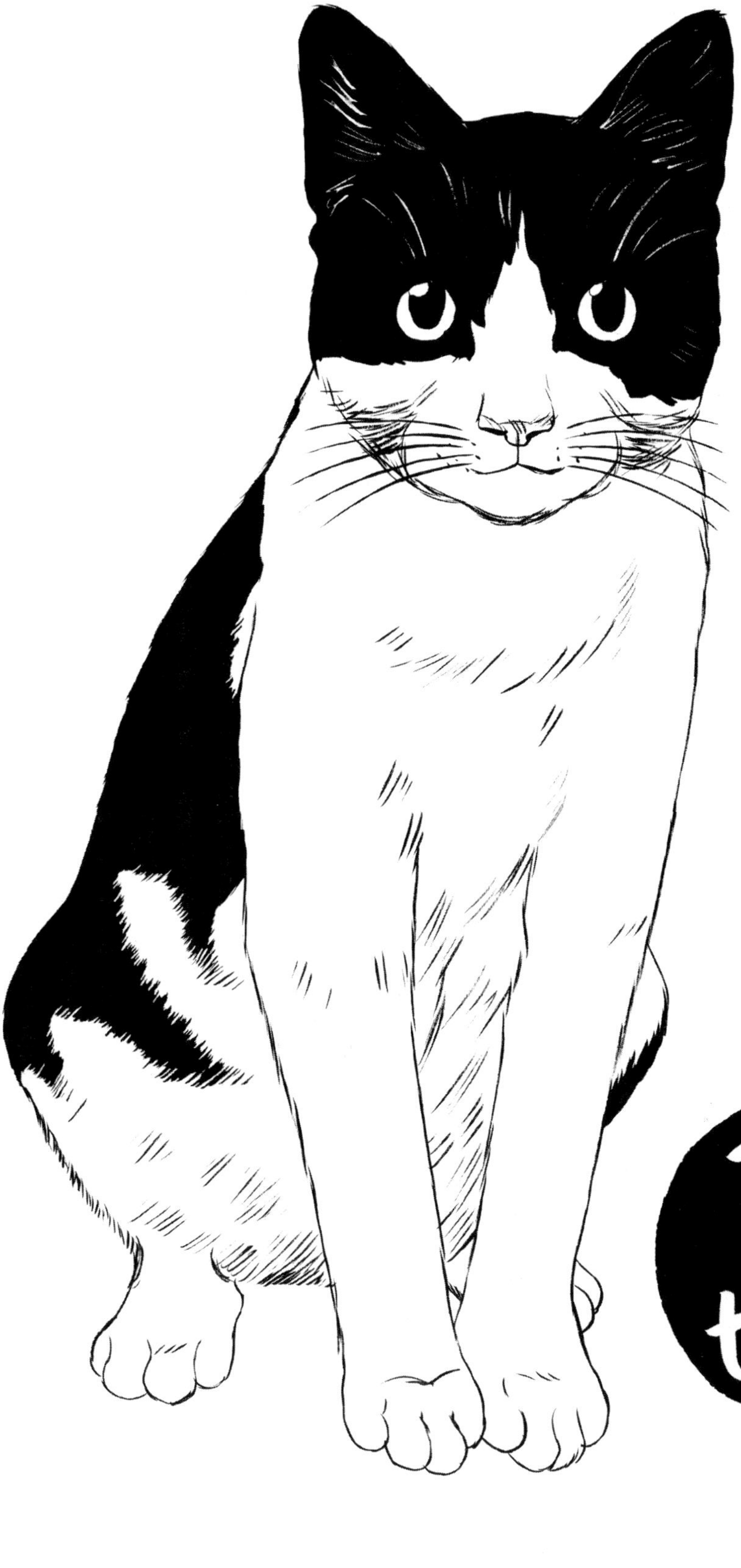

tim, it's time!

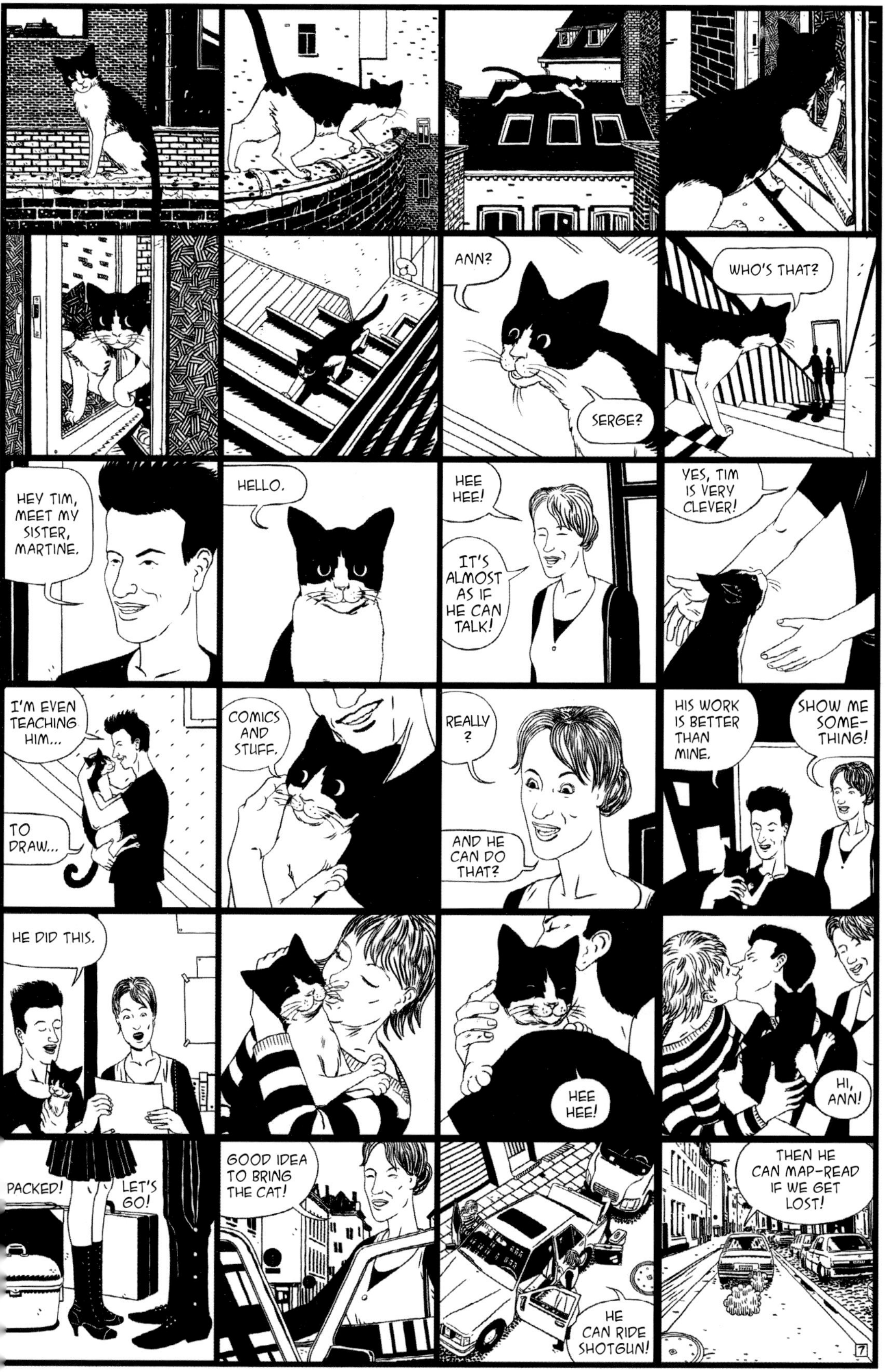
ANN?
SERGE?
WHO'S THAT?
HEY TIM, MEET MY SISTER, MARTINE.
HELLO.
HEE HEE!
IT'S ALMOST AS IF HE CAN TALK!
YES, TIM IS VERY CLEVER!
I'M EVEN TEACHING HIM...
TO DRAW...
COMICS AND STUFF.
REALLY?
AND HE CAN DO THAT?
HIS WORK IS BETTER THAN MINE.
SHOW ME SOME-THING!
HE DID THIS.
HEE HEE!
HI, ANN!
PACKED!
LET'S GO!
GOOD IDEA TO BRING THE CAT!
HE CAN RIDE SHOTGUN!
THEN HE CAN MAP-READ IF WE GET LOST!
7

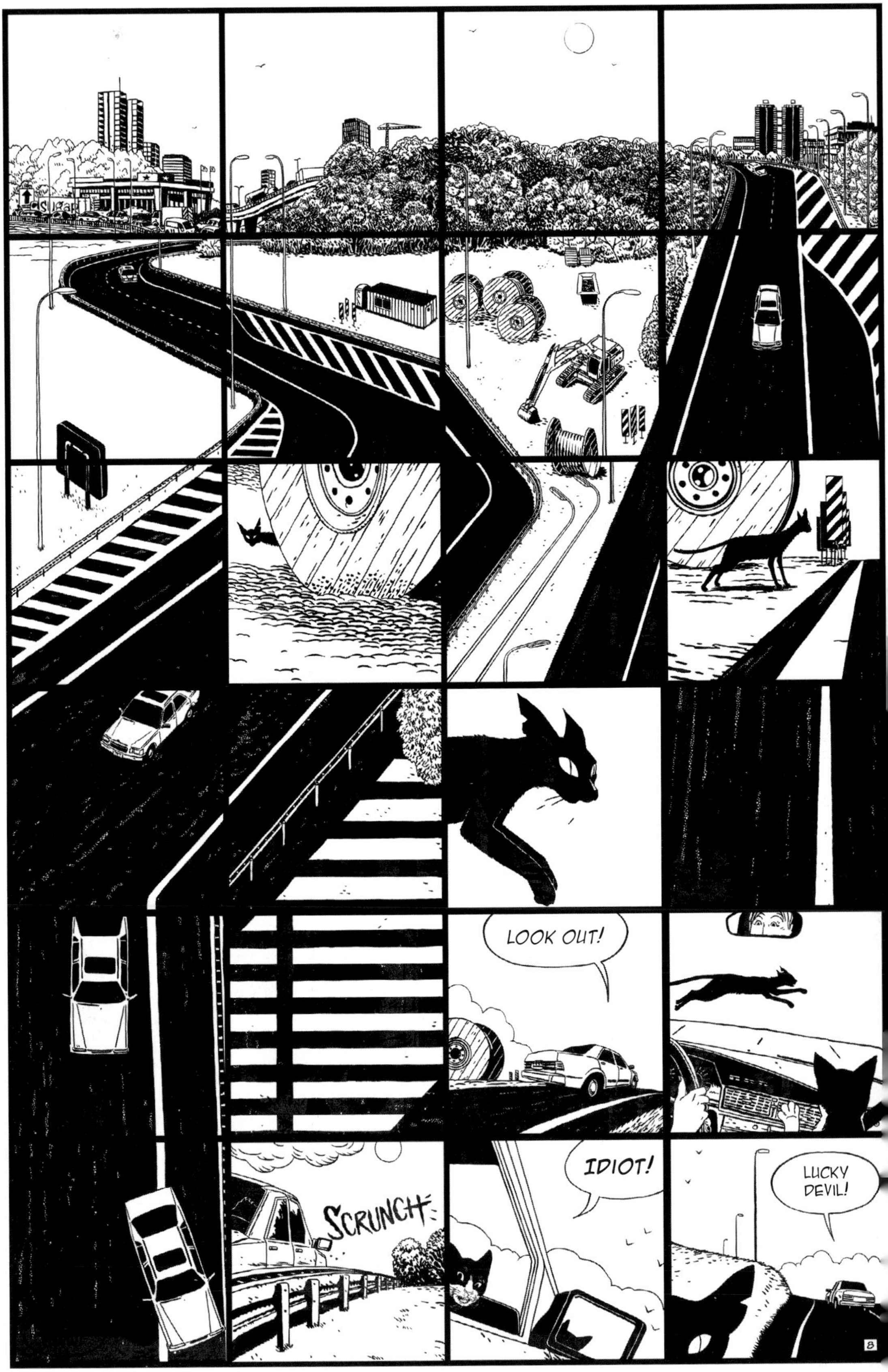
LOOK OUT!
SCRUNCH
IDIOT!
LUCKY DEVIL!
8

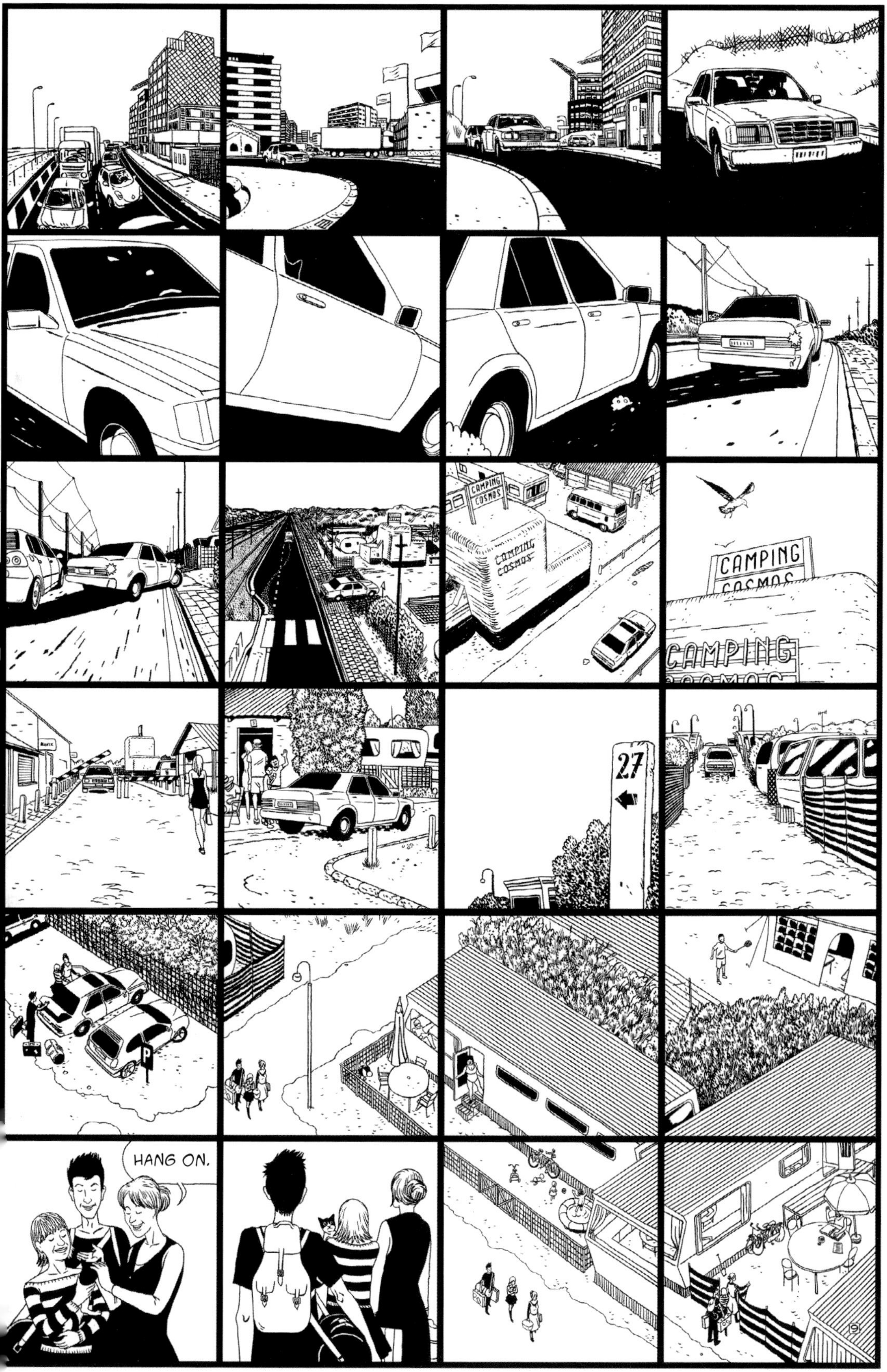
CAMPING
COSMOS
CAMPING
COSMOS
CAMPING
COSMOS
CAMPING
COSMOS
27
HANG ON.

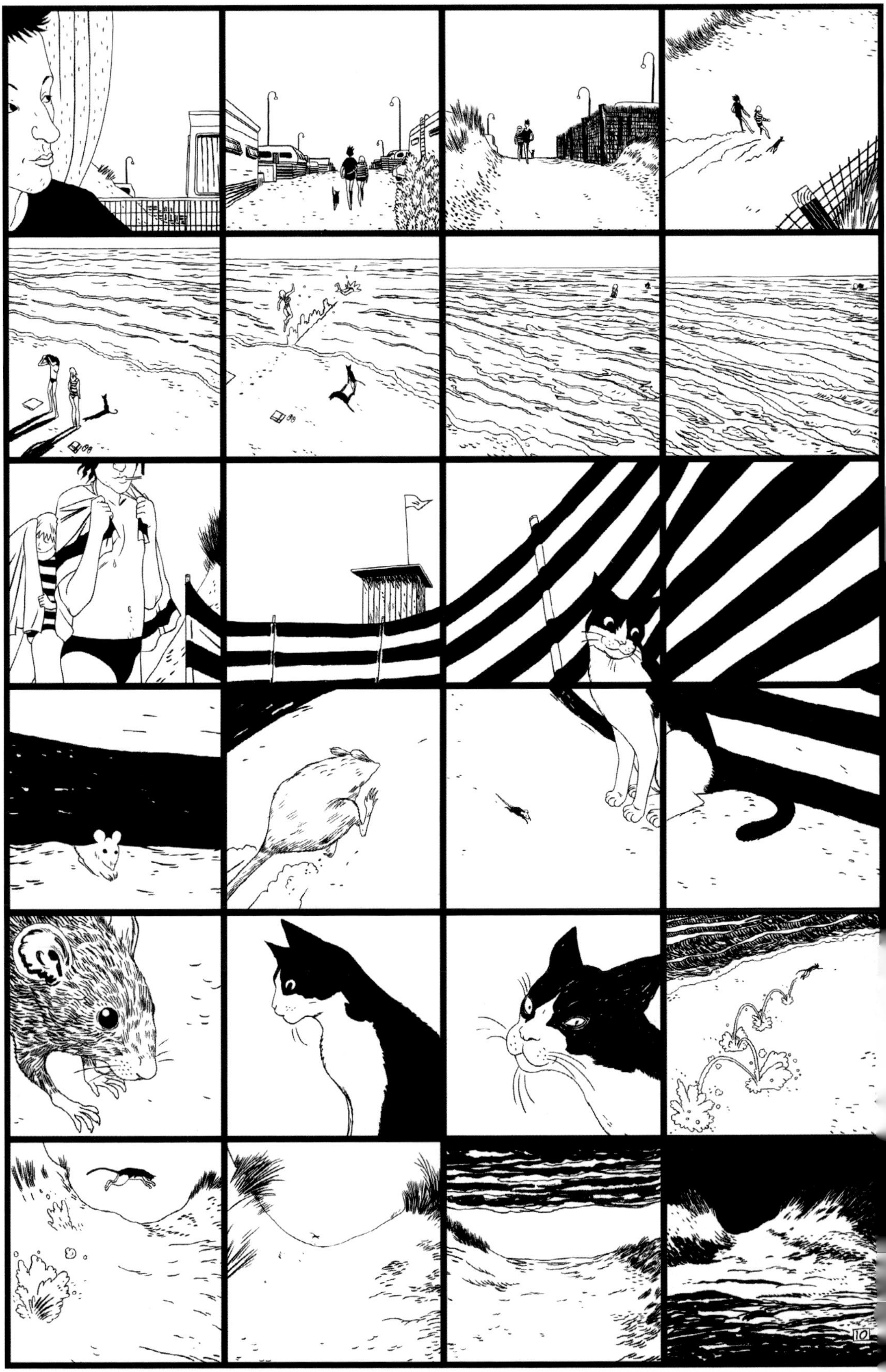

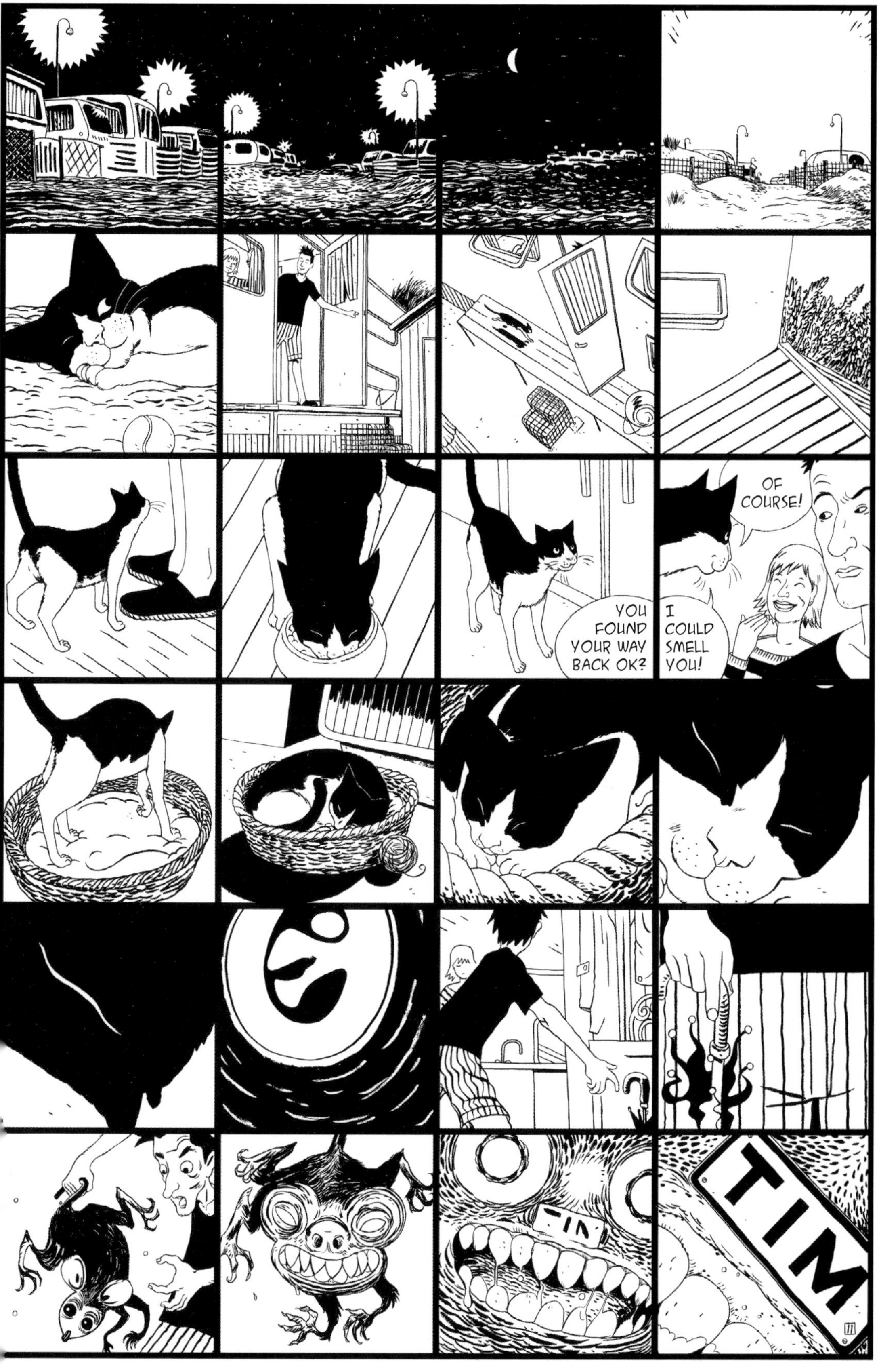
OF COURSE!
YOU FOUND YOUR WAY BACK OK?
I COULD SMELL YOU!
TIM
TIM

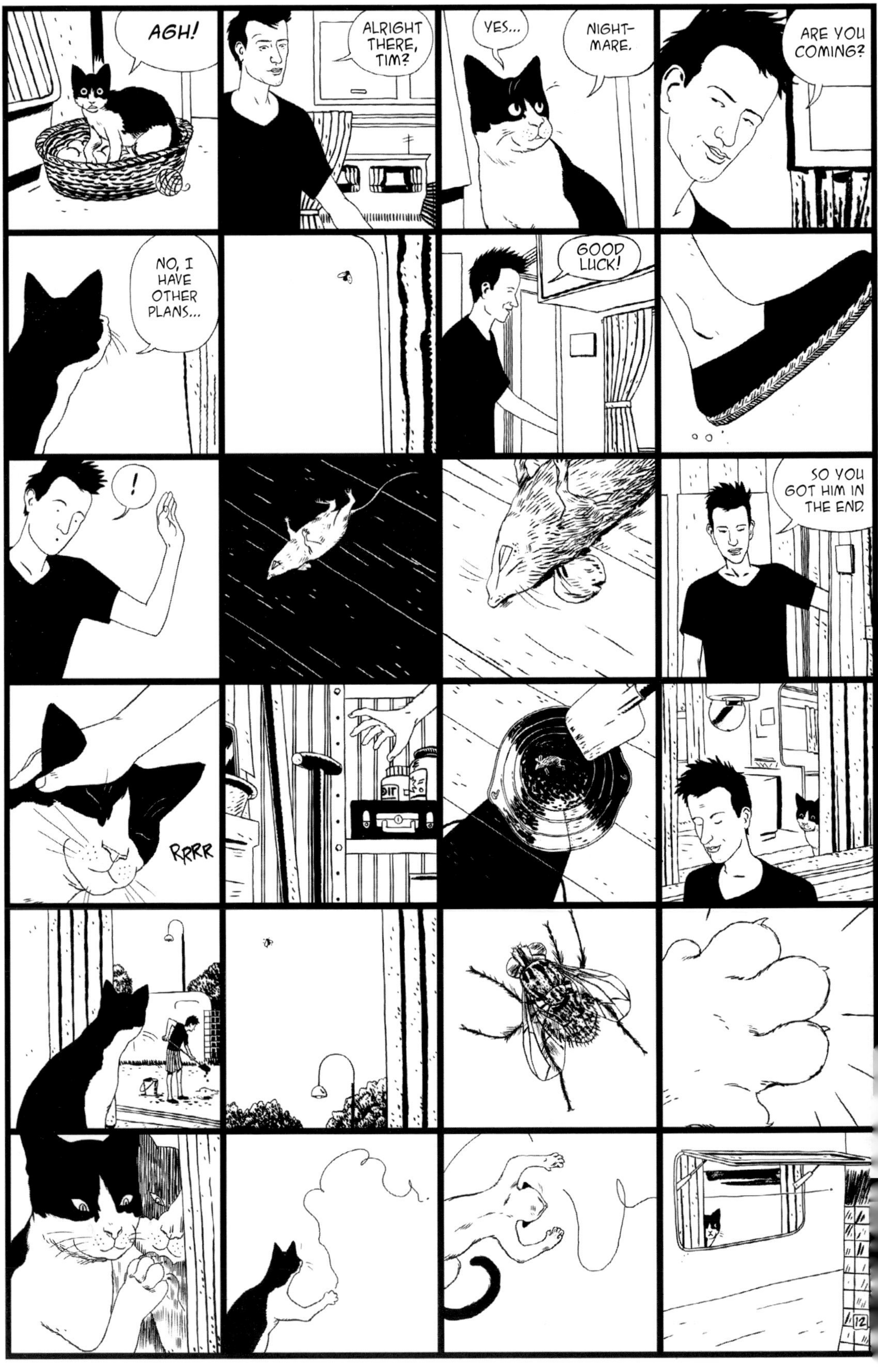
AGH!
ALRIGHT THERE, TIM?
YES...
NIGHT-MARE.
ARE YOU COMING?
NO, I HAVE OTHER PLANS...
GOOD LUCK!
!
SO YOU GOT HIM IN THE END.
RRRR
12

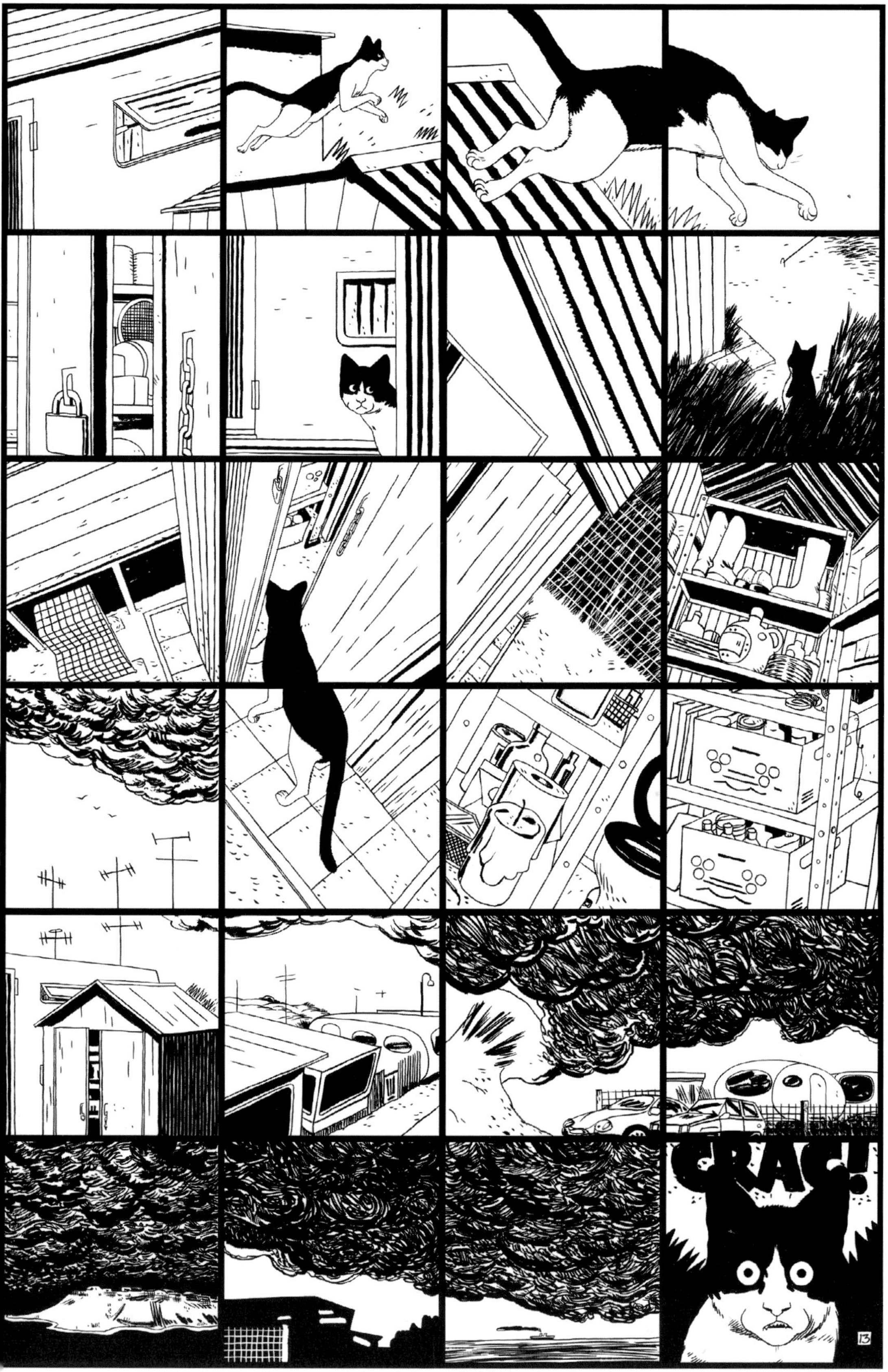
CRAC!

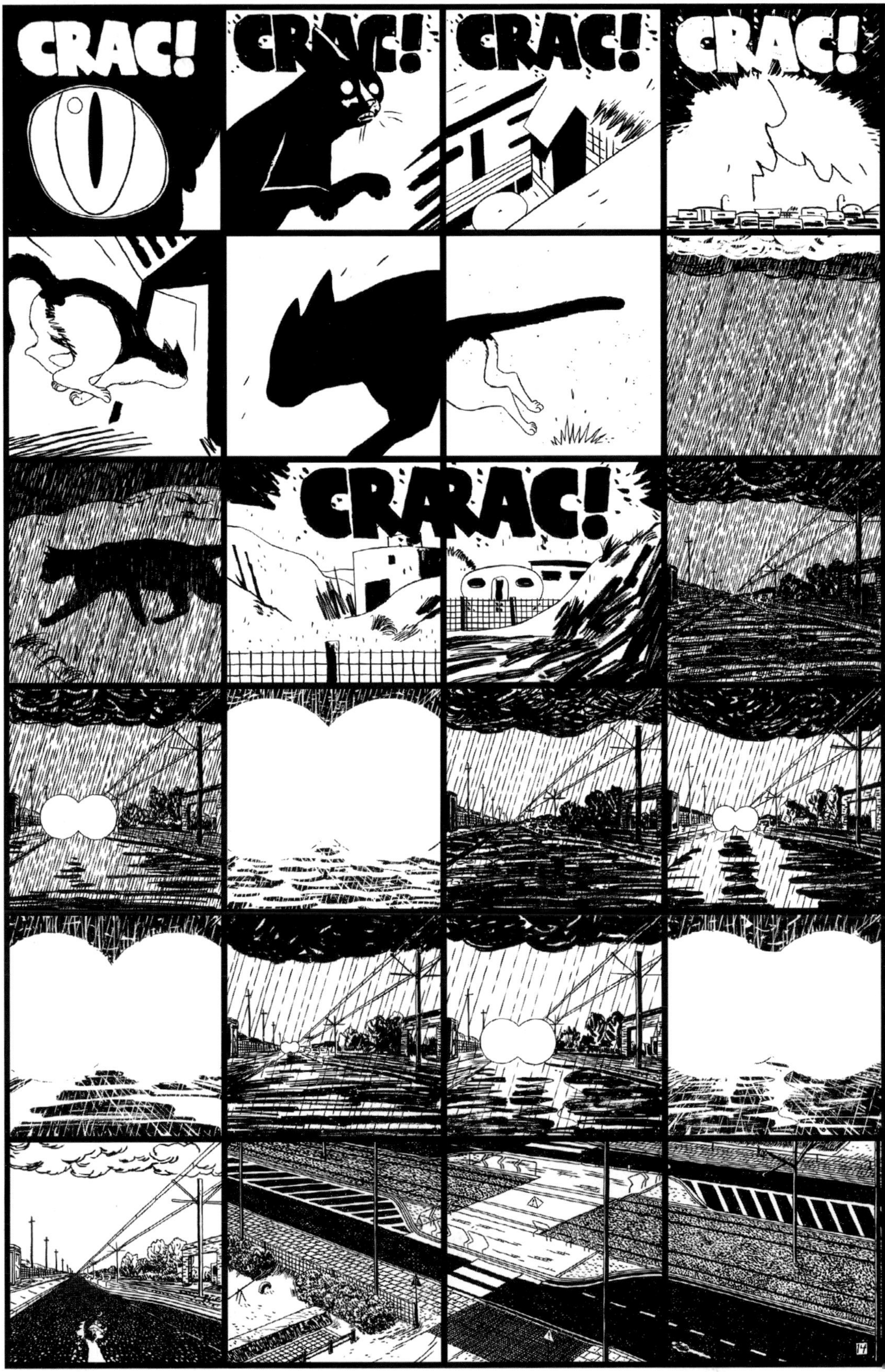
CRAC!
CRAC!
CRAC!
CRAC!
CRARAC!

just like jeffie

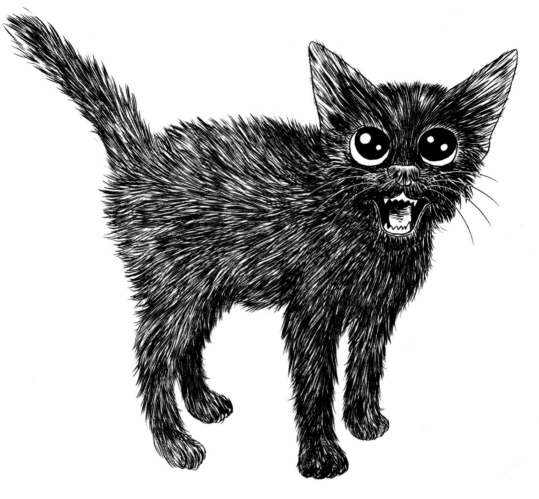

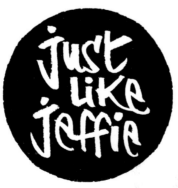

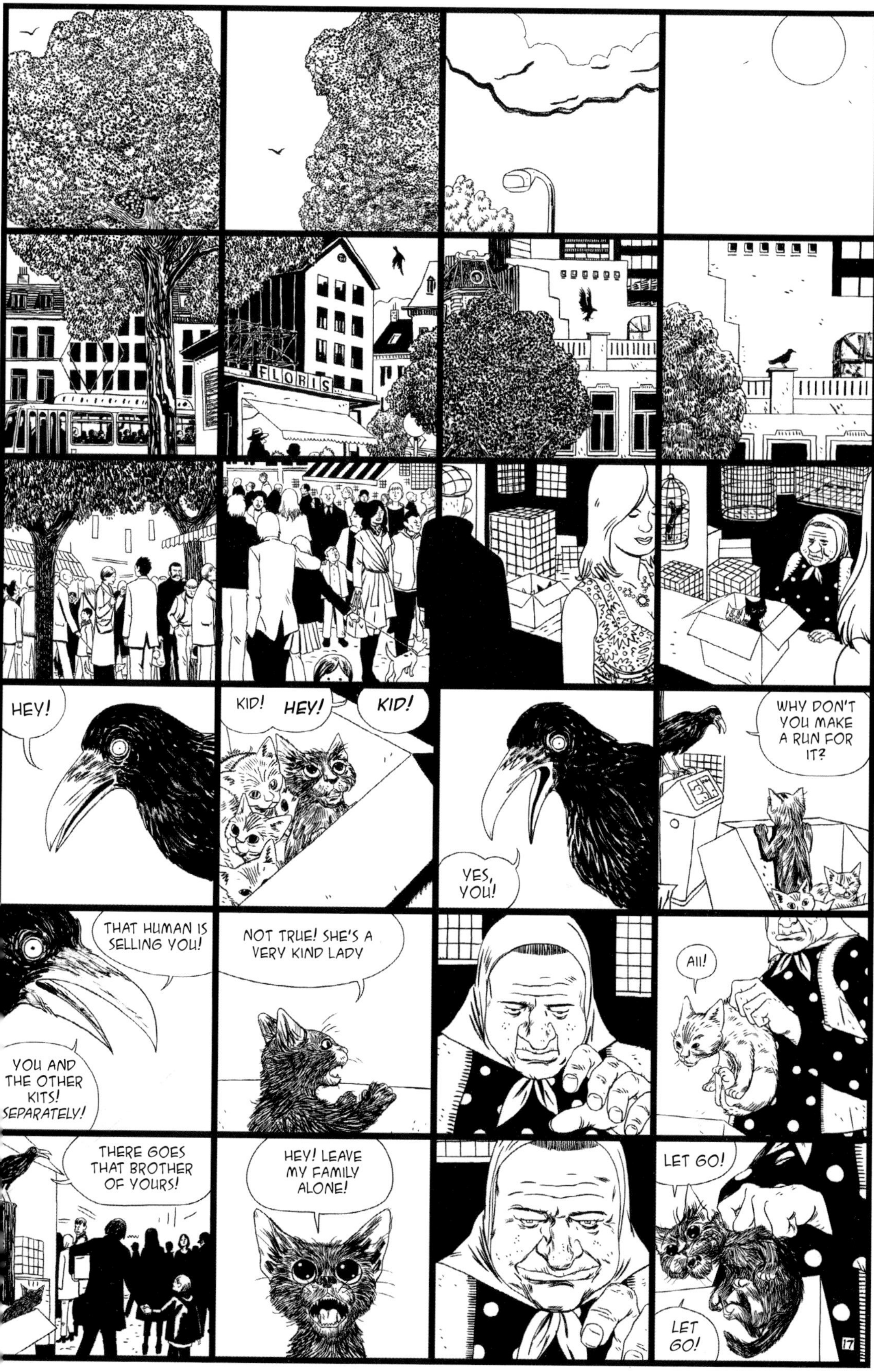
HEY!
KID!
HEY!
KID!
YES, YOU!
WHY DON'T YOU MAKE A RUN FOR IT?
THAT HUMAN IS SELLING YOU!
YOU AND THE OTHER KITS! SEPARATELY!
NOT TRUE! SHE'S A VERY KIND LADY
AII!
THERE GOES THAT BROTHER OF YOURS!
HEY! LEAVE MY FAMILY ALONE!
LET GO!
LET GO!
17

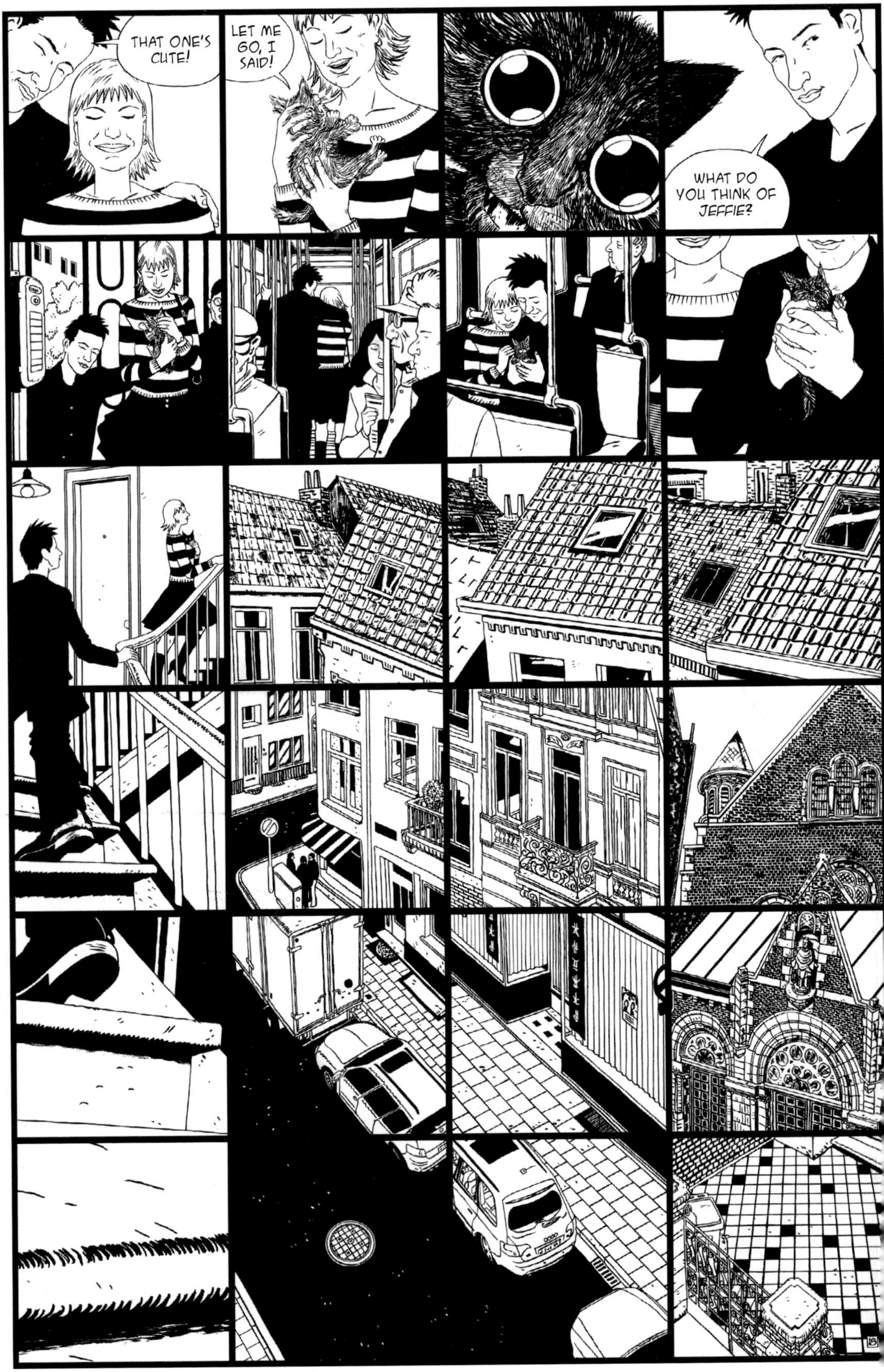
THAT ONE'S CUTE!
LET ME GO, I SAID!
WHAT DO YOU THINK OF JEFFIE?

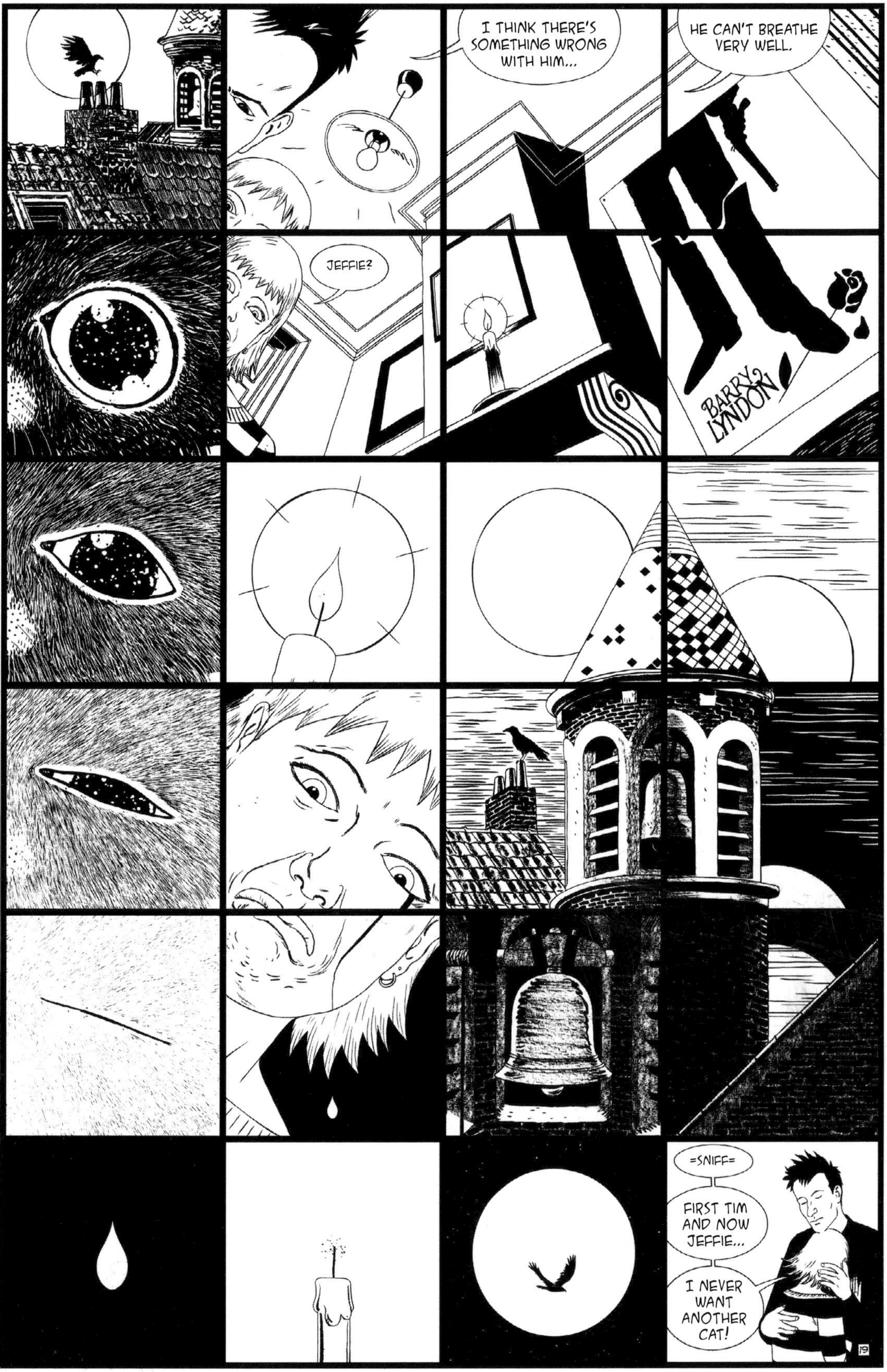
I THINK THERE'S SOMETHING WRONG WITH HIM...
HE CAN'T BREATHE VERY WELL.
JEFFIE?
BARRY LYNDON
=SNIFF=
FIRST TIM AND NOW JEFFIE...
I NEVER WANT ANOTHER CAT!
19

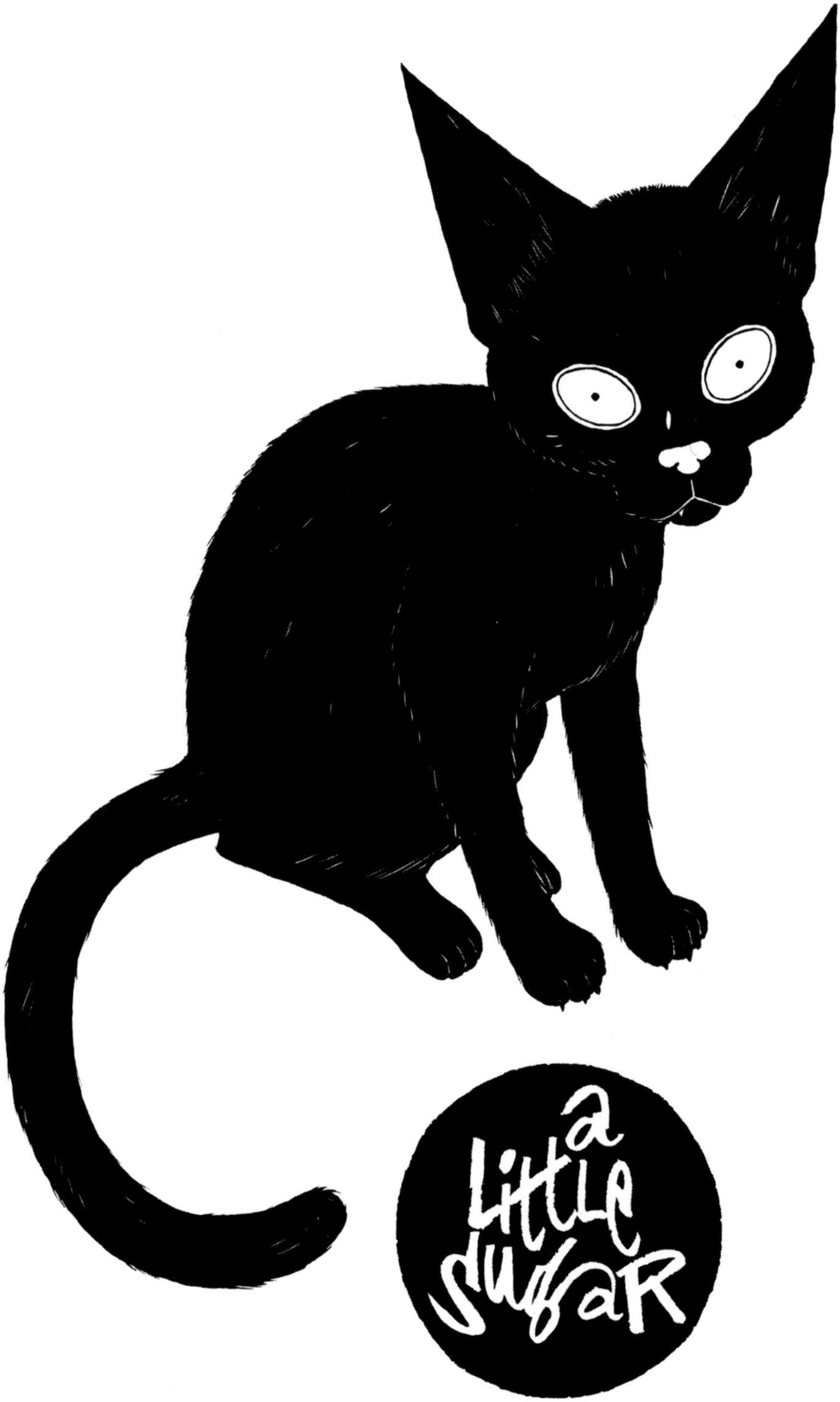
a little sugar

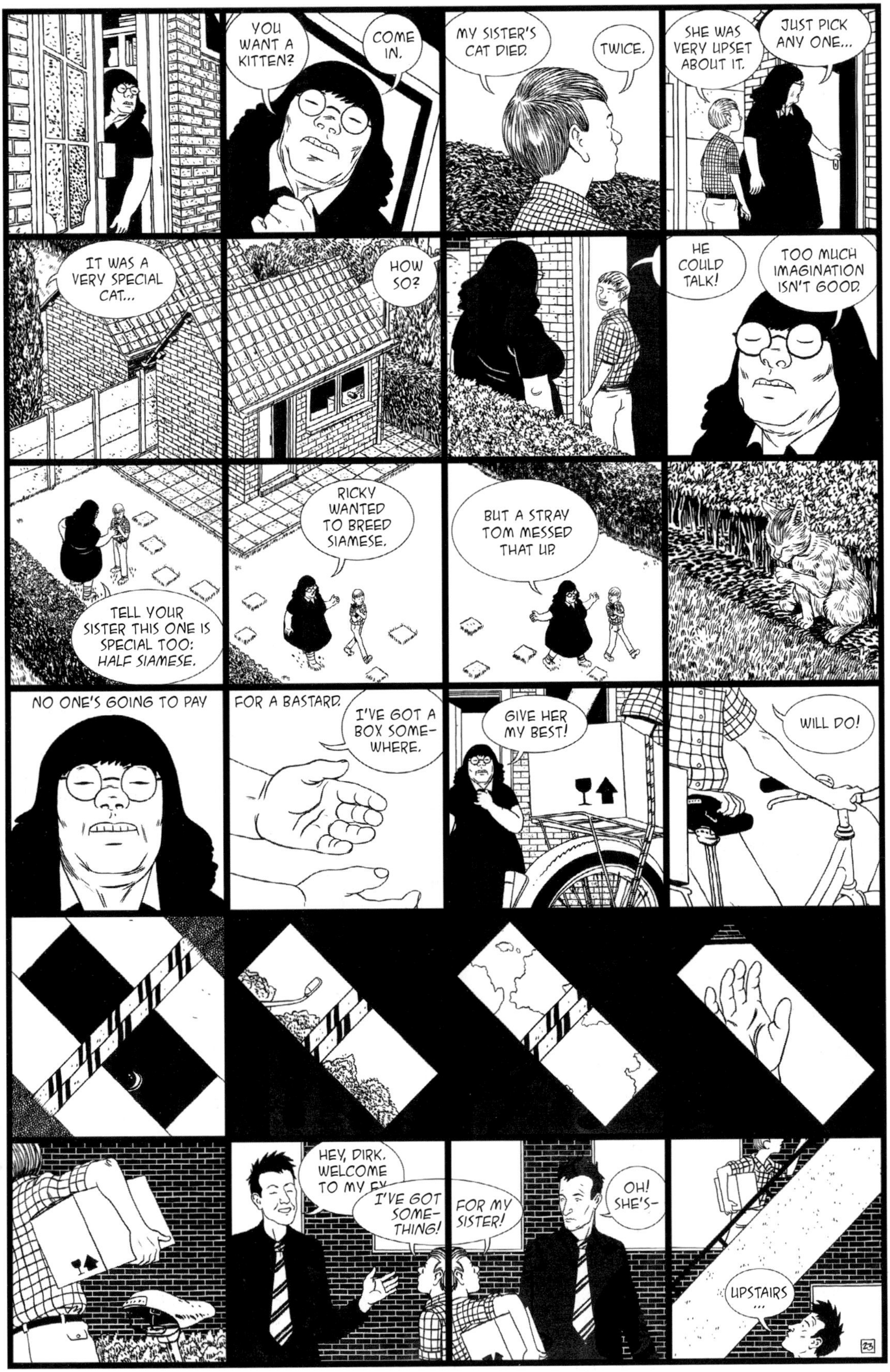
YOU WANT A KITTEN?
COME IN.
MY SISTER'S CAT DIED.
TWICE.
SHE WAS VERY UPSET ABOUT IT.
JUST PICK ANY ONE...
IT WAS A VERY SPECIAL CAT...
HOW SO?
HE COULD TALK!
TOO MUCH IMAGINATION ISN'T GOOD.
TELL YOUR SISTER THIS ONE IS SPECIAL TOO: HALF SIAMESE.
RICKY WANTED TO BREED SIAMESE.
BUT A STRAY TOM MESSED THAT UP.
NO ONE'S GOING TO PAY
FOR A BASTARD.
I'VE GOT A BOX SOMEWHERE.
GIVE HER MY BEST!
WILL DO!
HEY, DIRK. WELCOME TO MY EX
I'VE GOT SOMETHING!
FOR MY SISTER!
OH! SHE'S-
UPSTAIRS...
23

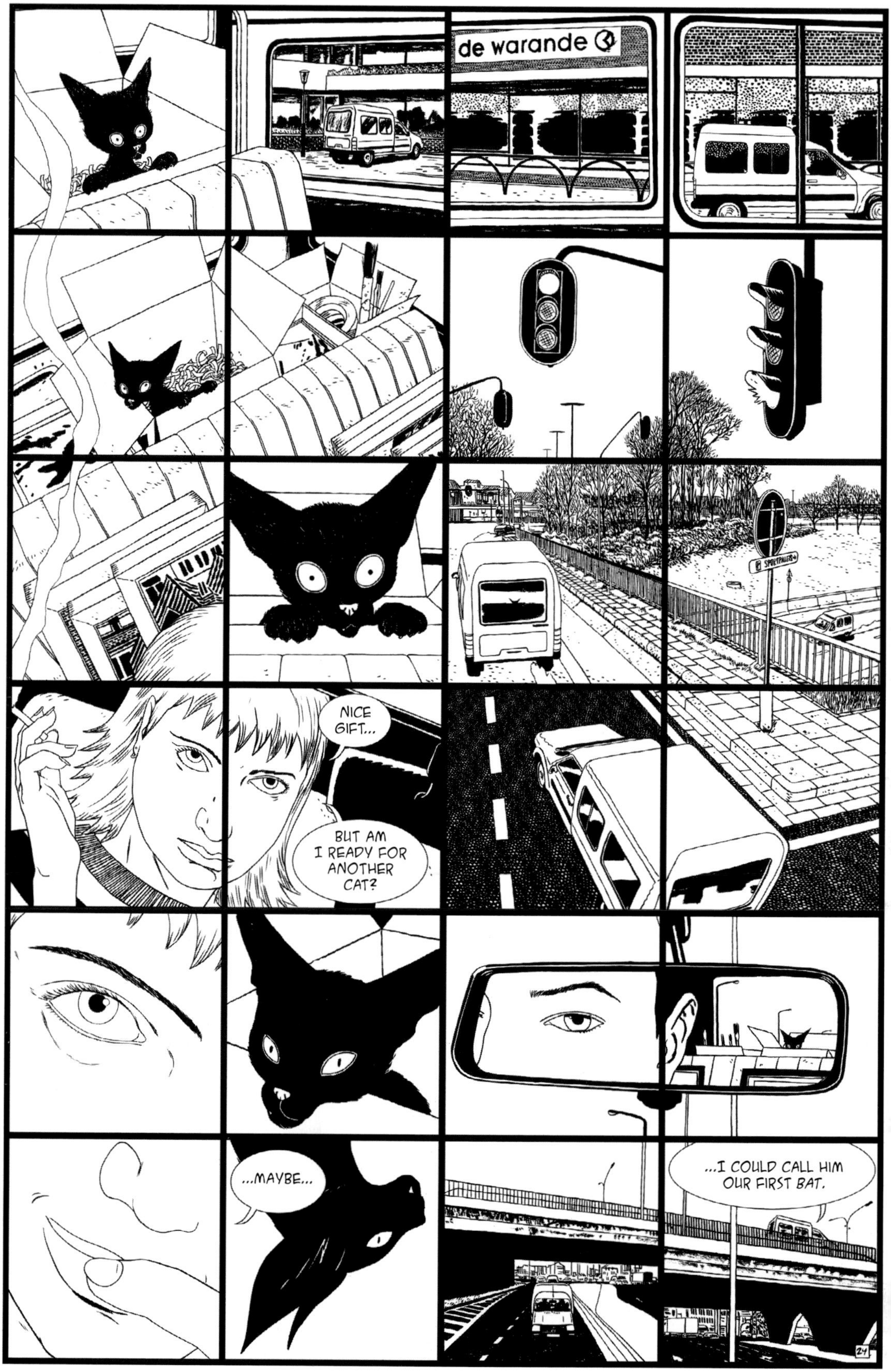
de warande
SPORTPALEIS
NICE GIFT...
BUT AM I READY FOR ANOTHER CAT?
...MAYBE...
...I COULD CALL HIM OUR FIRST BAT.
24

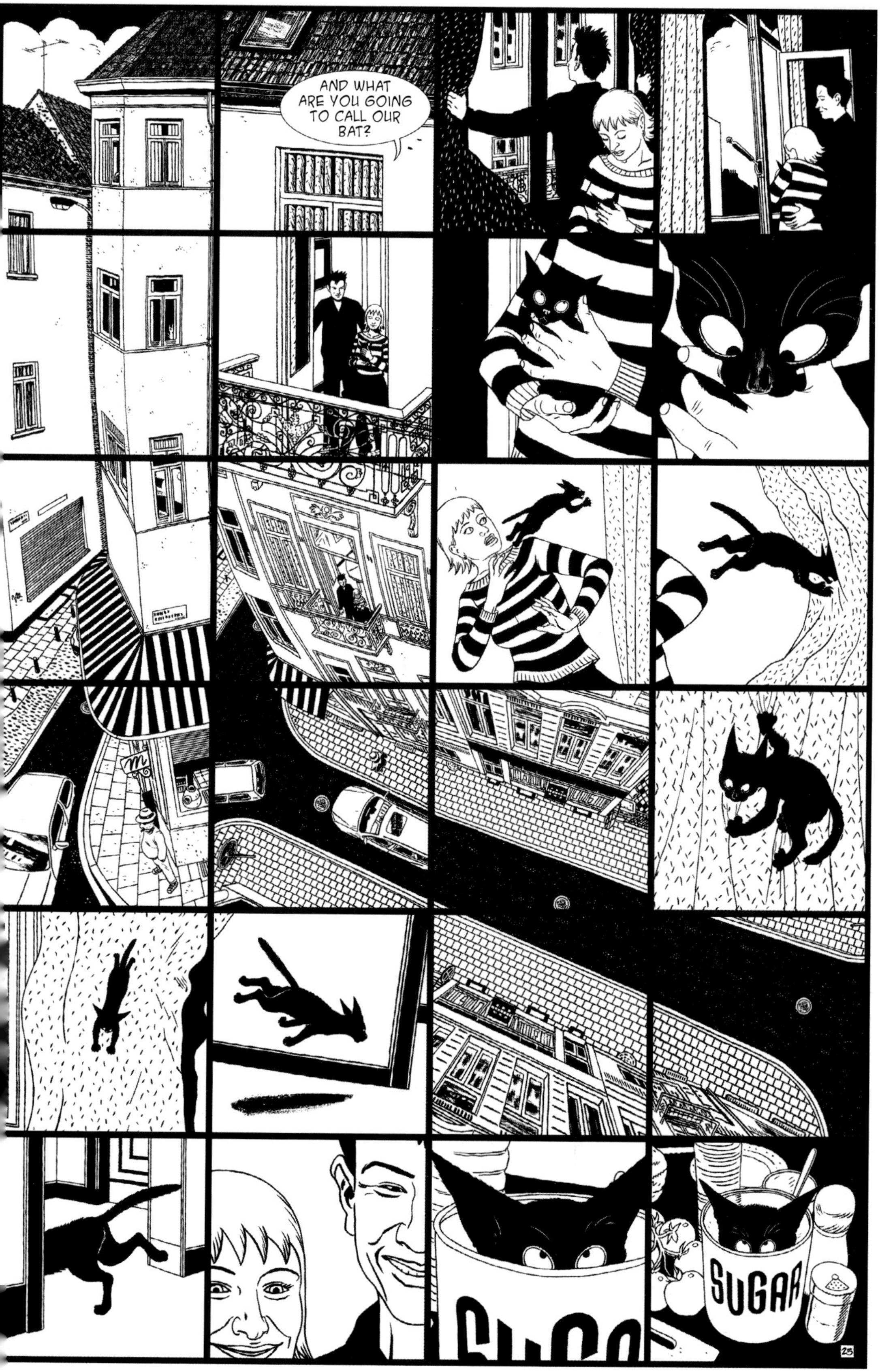
AND WHAT ARE YOU GOING TO CALL OUR BAT?
SUGAR
SUGA

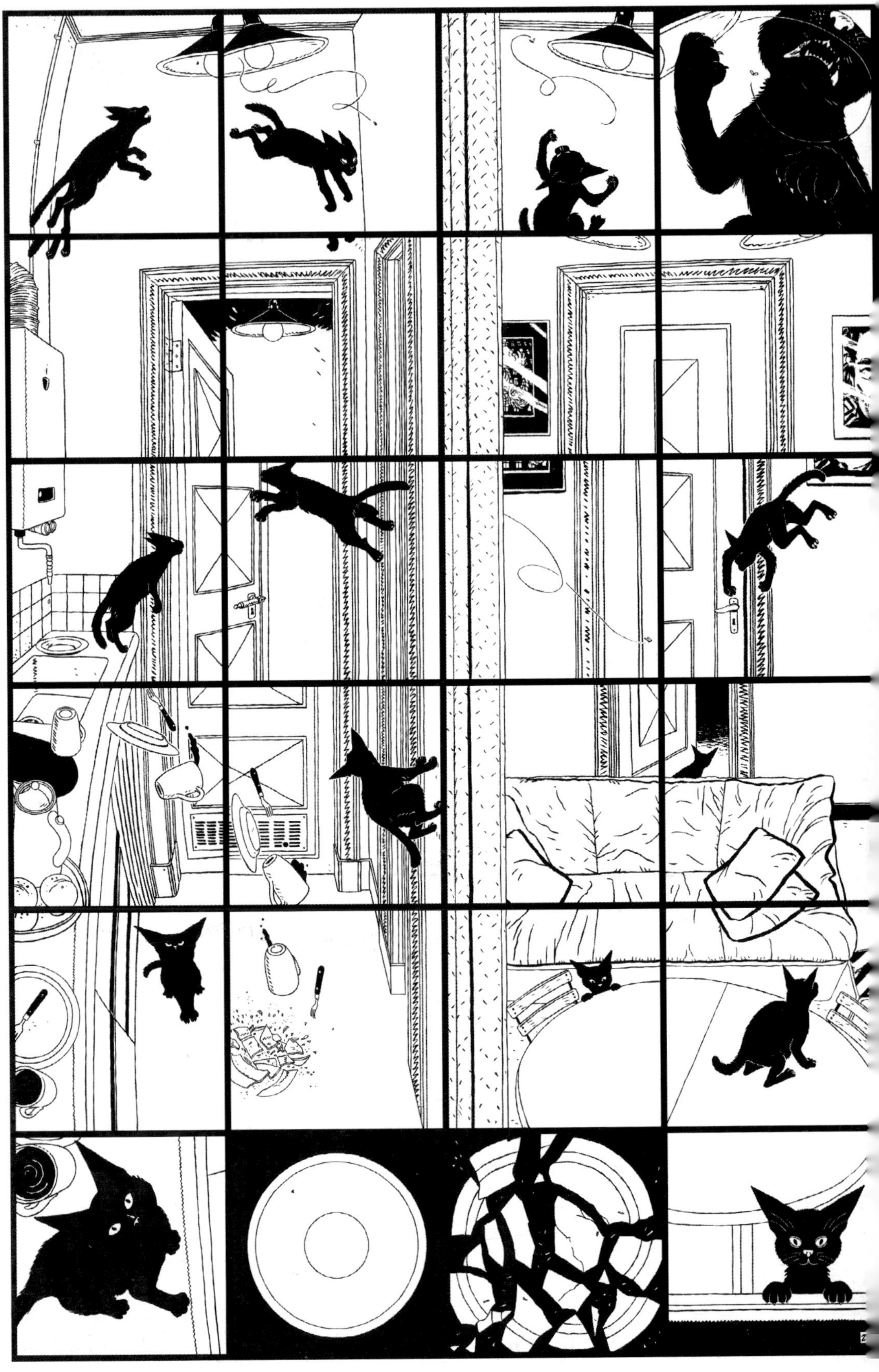

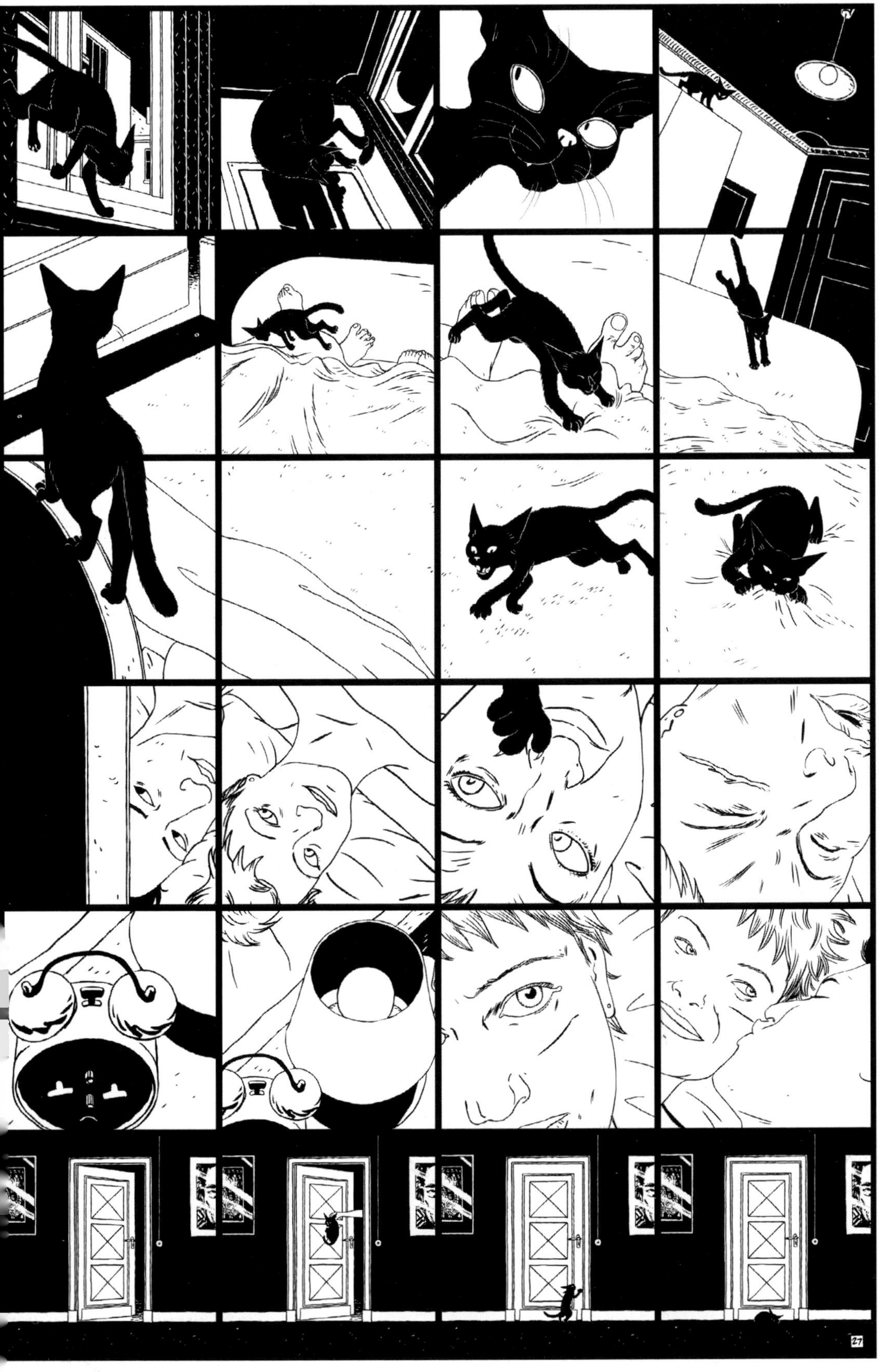

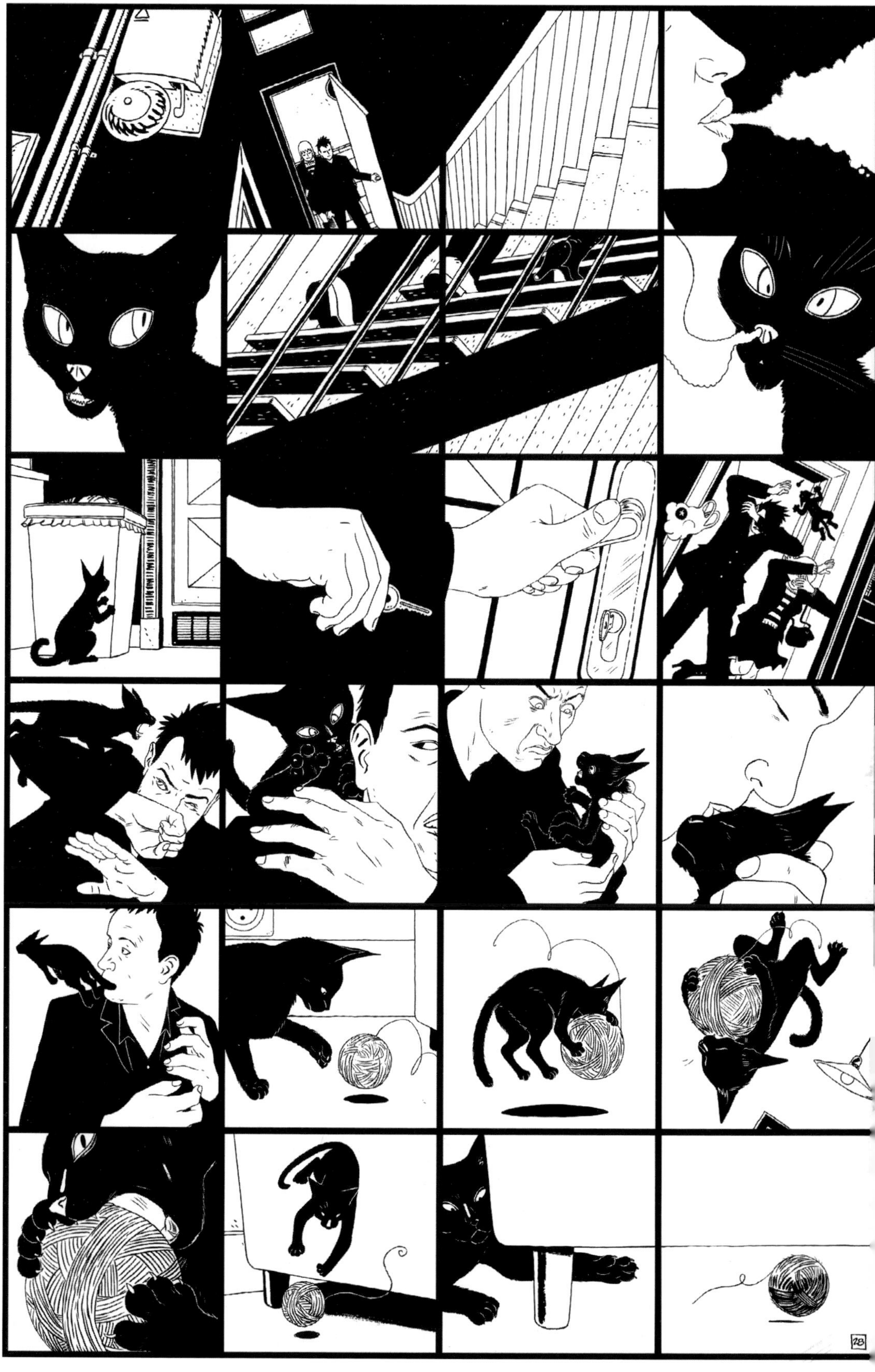

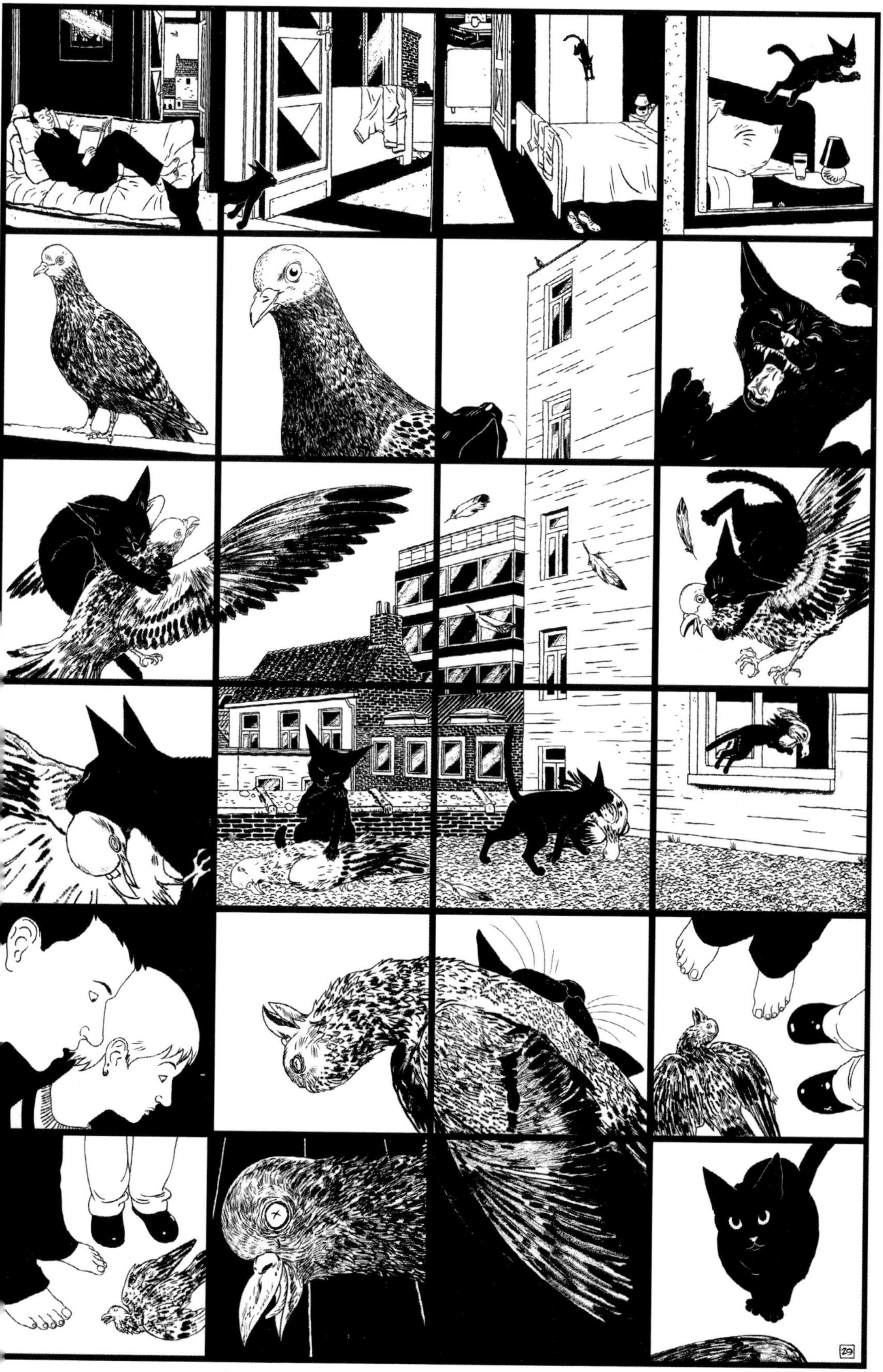

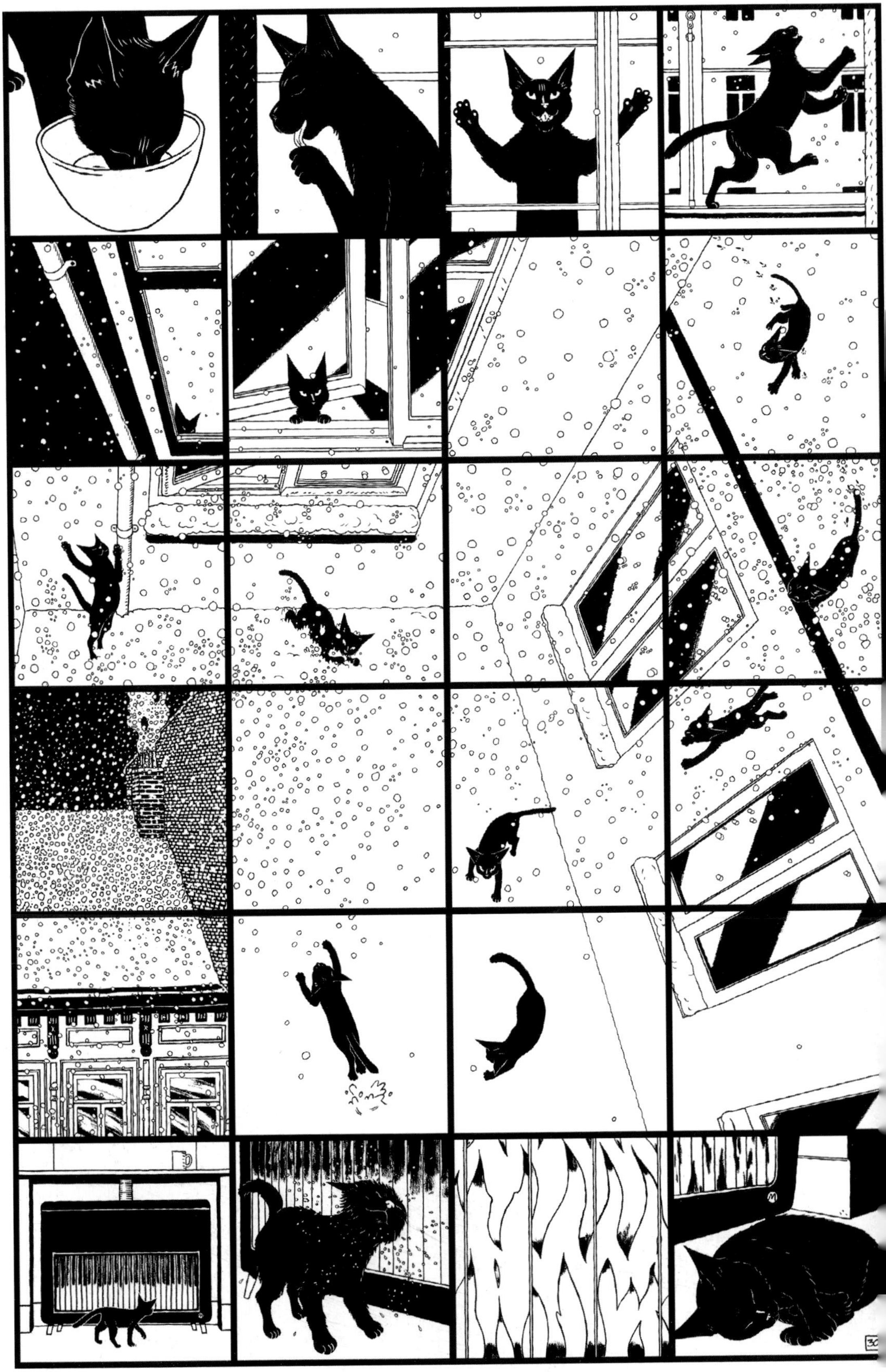

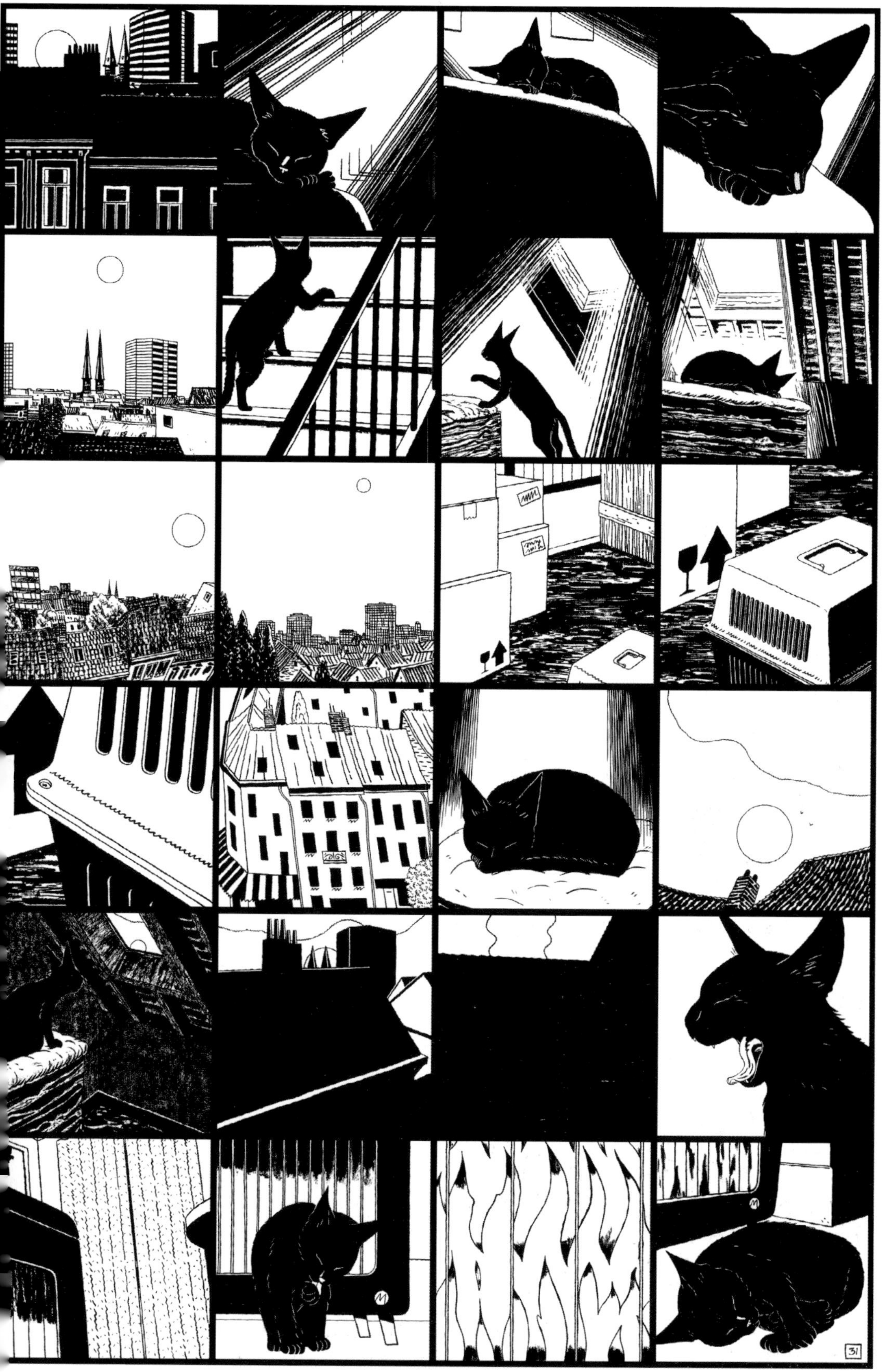
31

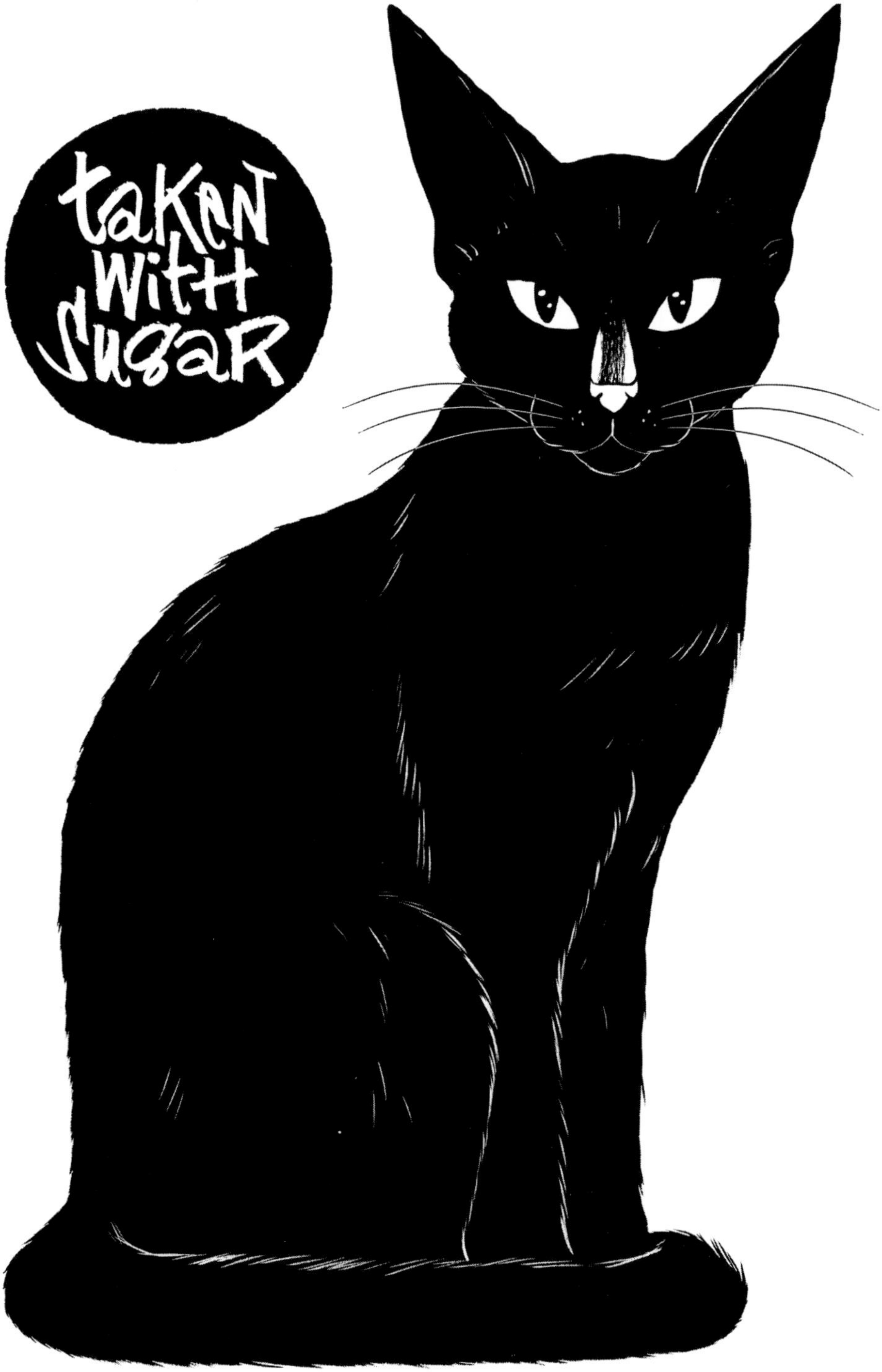
taken with sugar

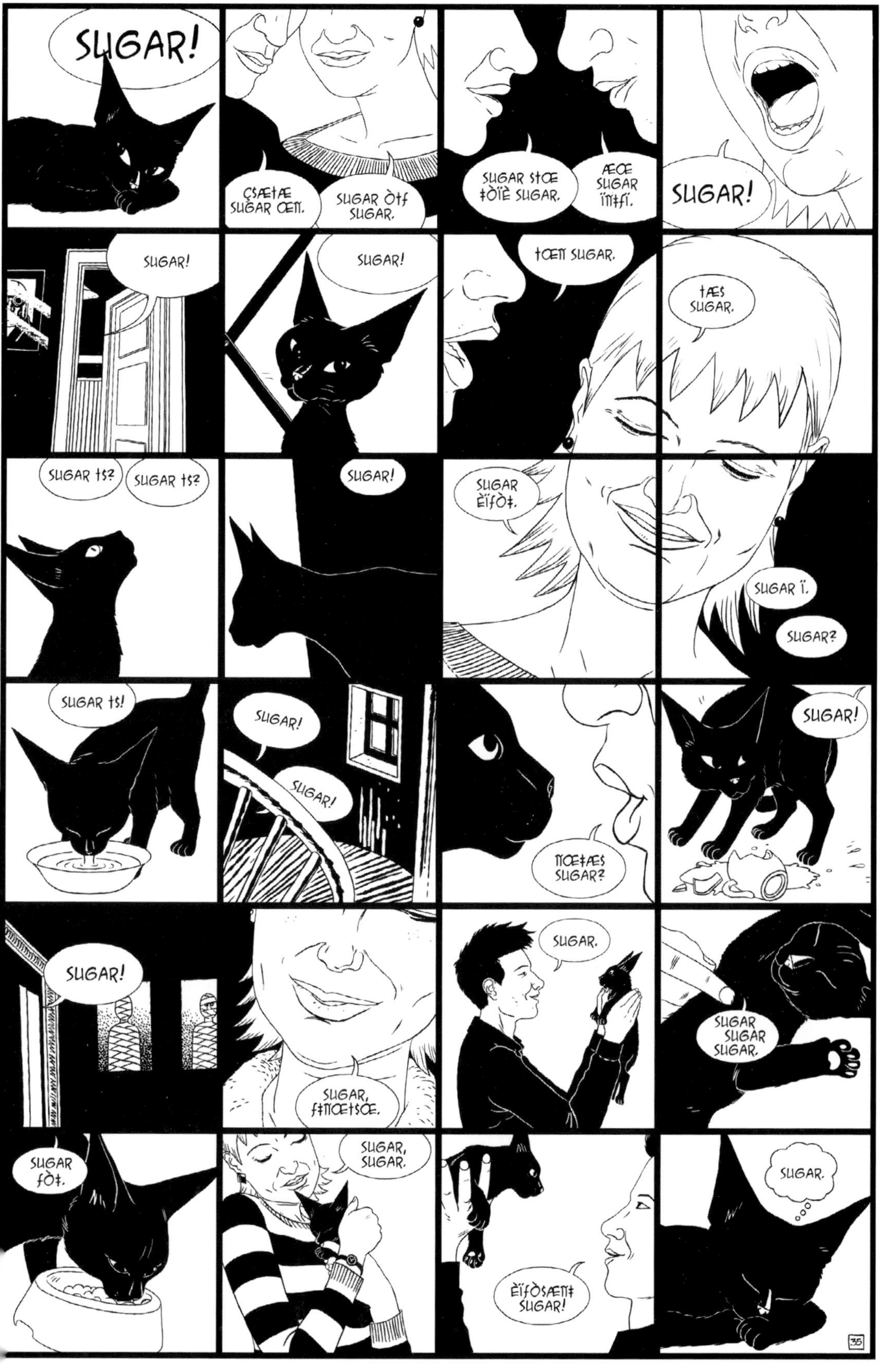
SUGAR!
ÇSÆ‡Æ SUGAR ŒΠ.
SUGAR Ò‡ƒ SUGAR.
SUGAR $‡Œ ‡ÖÏÈ SUGAR.
ÆŒ SUGAR ÏΠ‡ƒÏ.
SUGAR!
SUGAR!
SUGAR!
‡ŒΠ SUGAR.
‡Æ$ SUGAR.
SUGAR ‡$?
SUGAR ‡$?
SUGAR!
SUGAR ÈÏƒÒ‡.
SUGAR Ï.
SUGAR?
SUGAR ‡$!
SUGAR!
SUGAR!
ΠŒ‡Æ$ SUGAR?
SUGAR!
SUGAR!
SUGAR, ƒ‡ΠŒ‡$Œ.
SUGAR.
SUGAR SUGAR SUGAR.
SUGAR ƒÒ‡.
SUGAR, SUGAR.
ÈÏƒÒ$ÆΠ‡ SUGAR!
SUGAR.

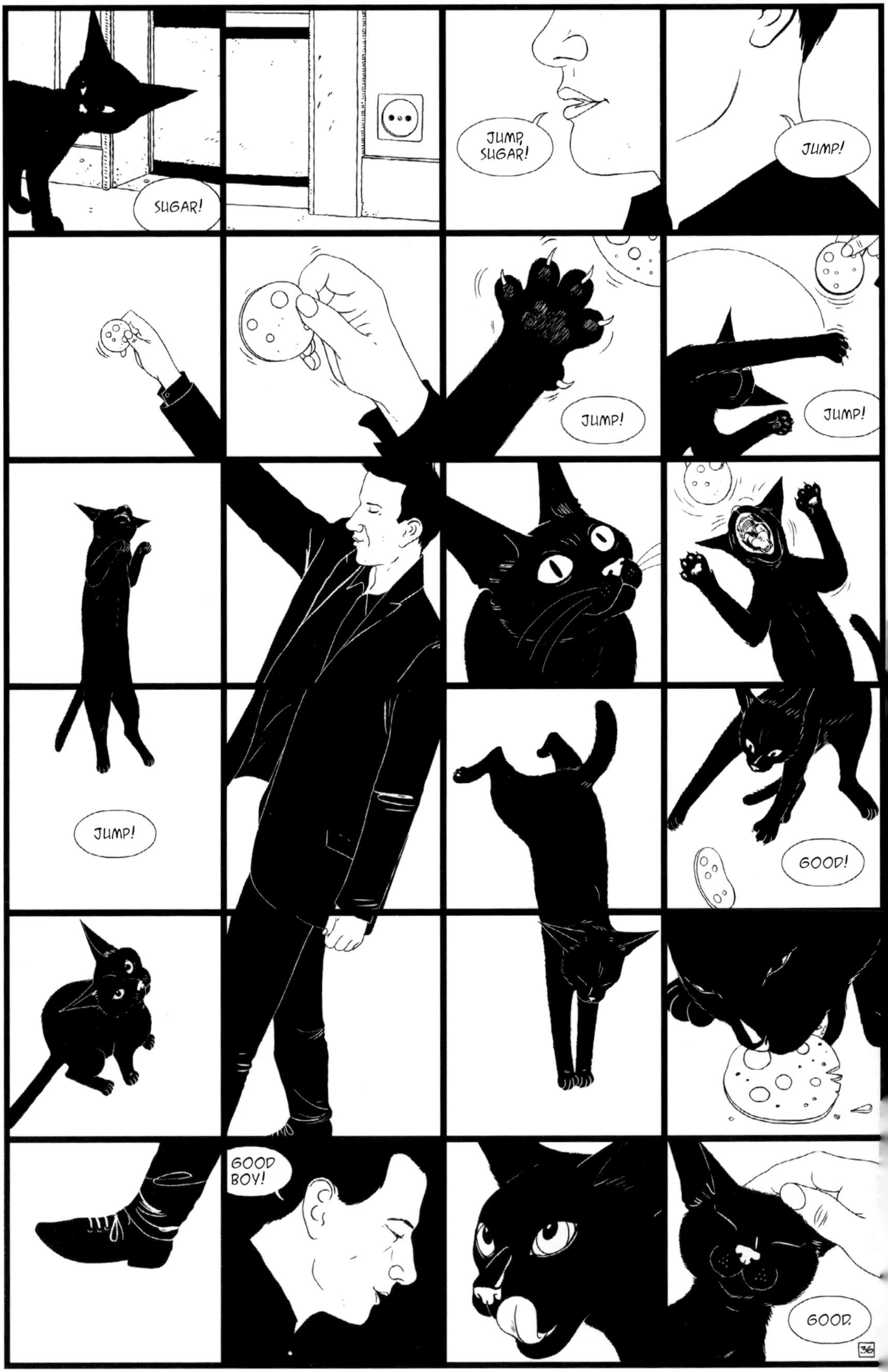
SUGAR!
JUMP, SUGAR!
JUMP!
JUMP!
JUMP!
JUMP!
GOOD!
GOOD BOY!
GOOD.
36

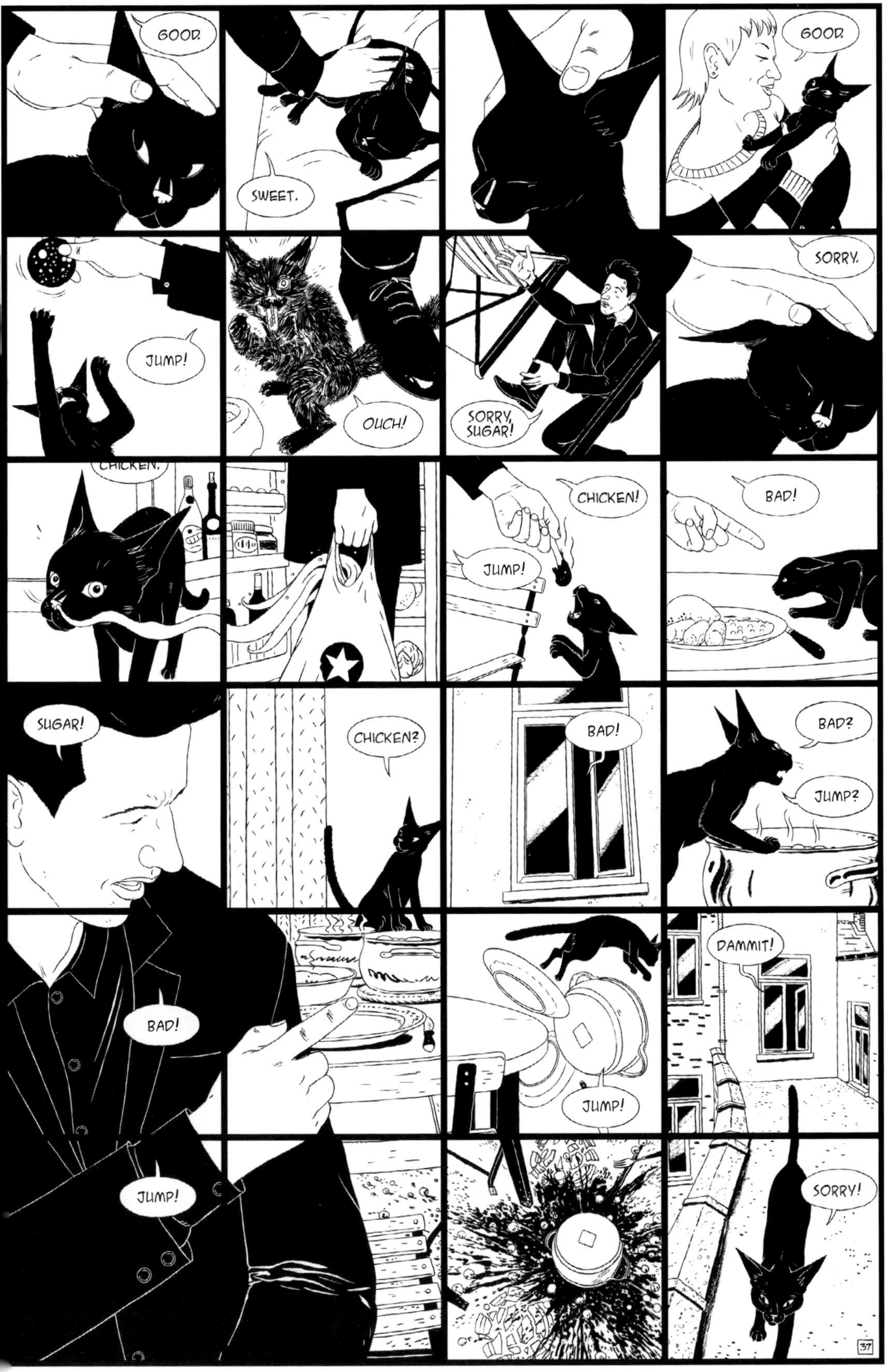
GOOD.
SWEET.
GOOD.
JUMP!
OUCH!
SORRY, SUGAR!
SORRY.
CHICKEN.
CHICKEN!
JUMP!
BAD!
SUGAR!
CHICKEN?
BAD!
BAD?
JUMP?
BAD!
JUMP!
DAMMIT!
JUMP!
SORRY!

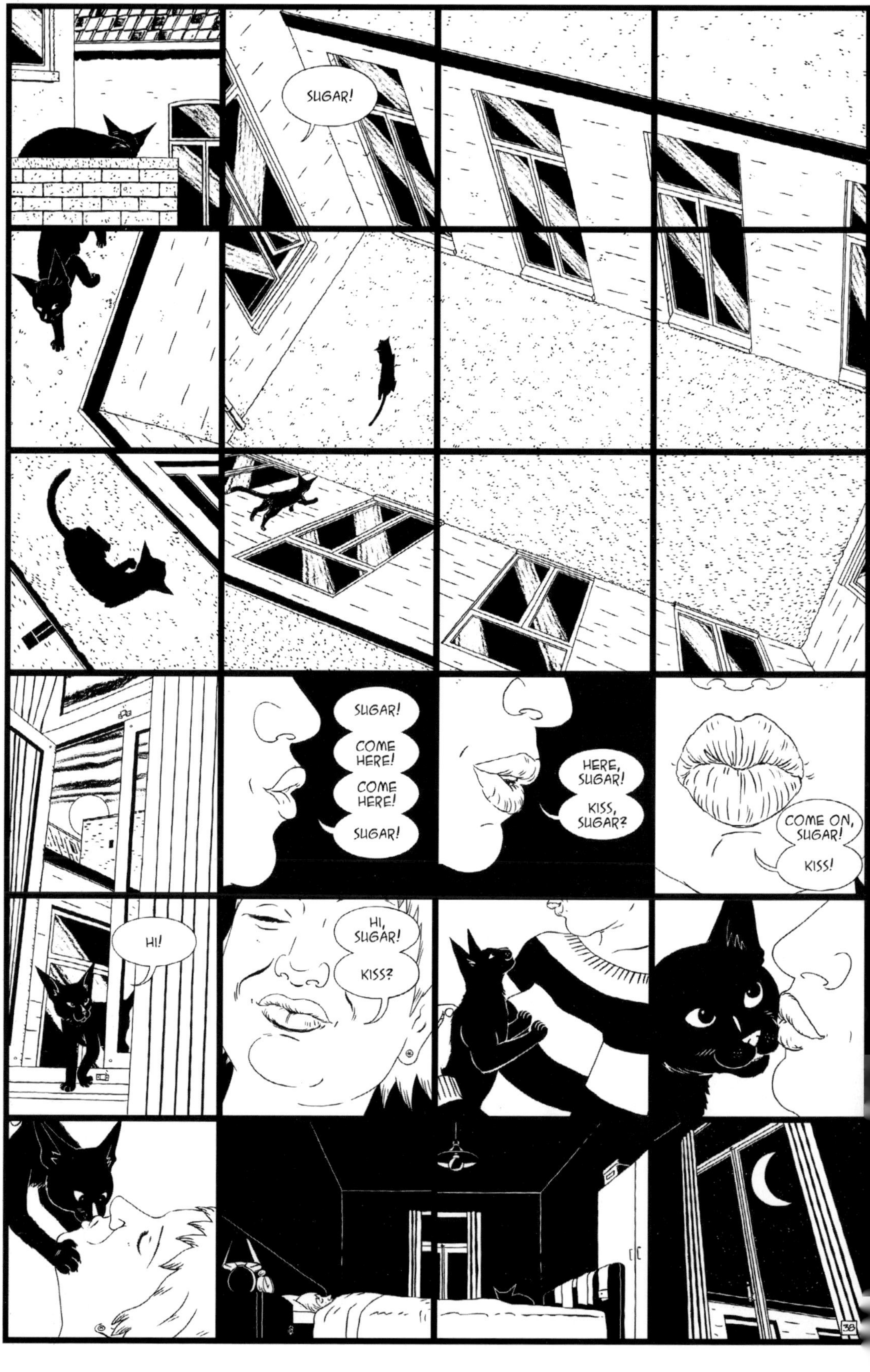

SUGAR!
SUGAR!
COME HERE!
COME HERE!
SUGAR!
HERE, SUGAR!
KISS, SUGAR?
COME ON, SUGAR!
KISS!
HI!
HI, SUGAR!
KISS?

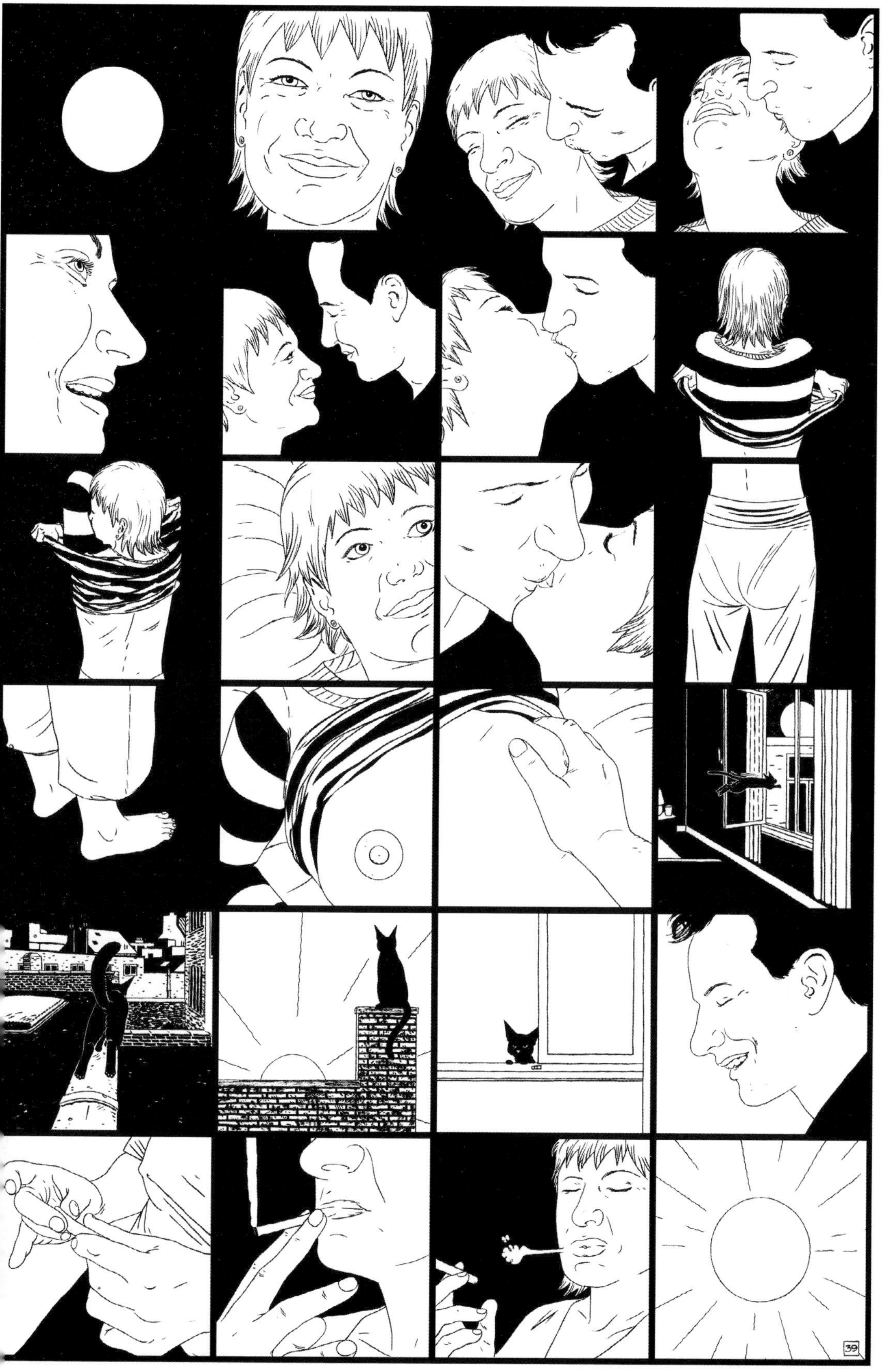

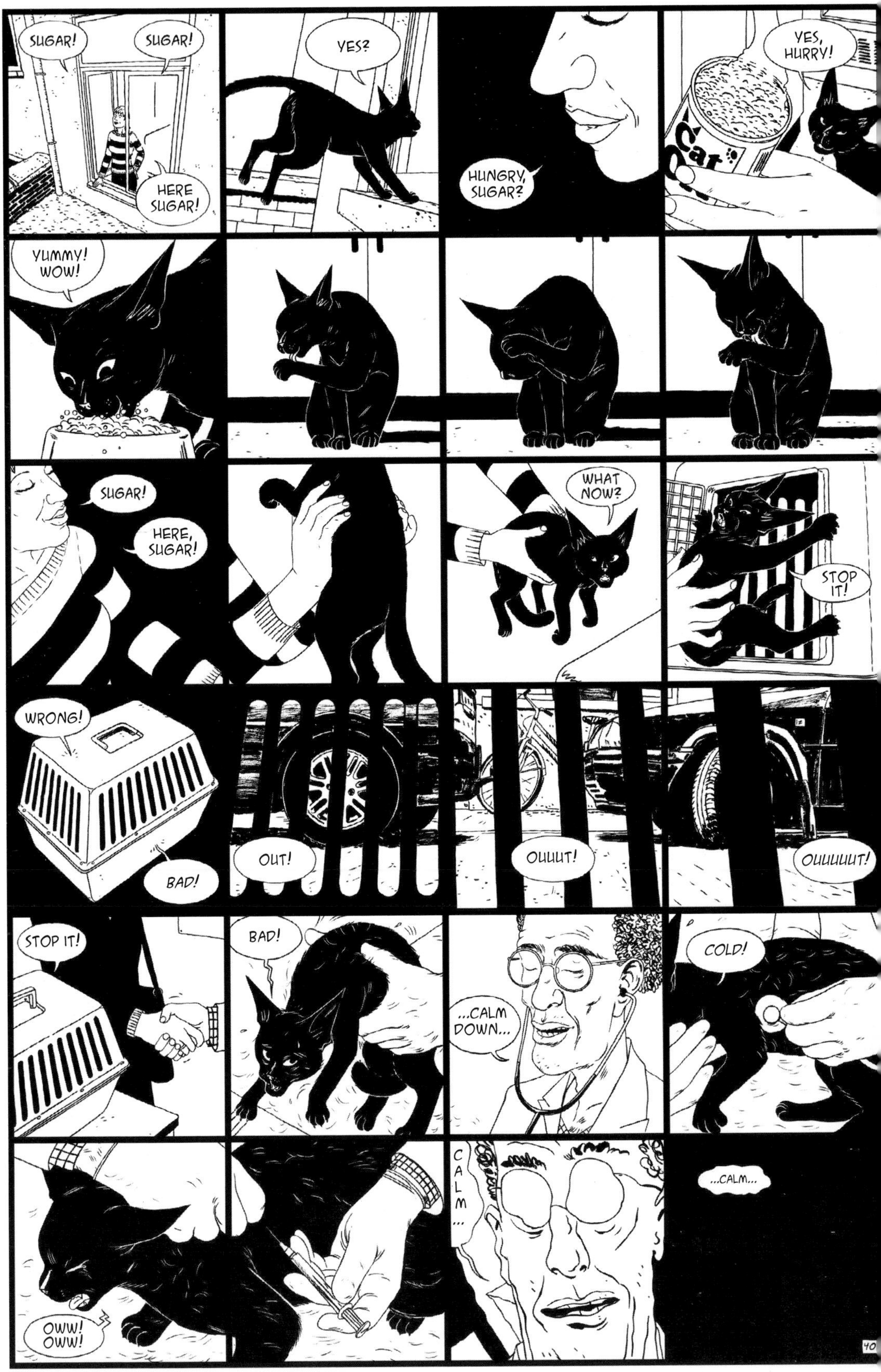
SUGAR!
SUGAR!
HERE SUGAR!
YES?
HUNGRY, SUGAR?
YES, HURRY!
Cat
YUMMY! WOW!
SUGAR!
HERE, SUGAR!
WHAT NOW?
STOP IT!
WRONG!
BAD!
OUT!
OUUUT!
OUUUUUT!
STOP IT!
BAD!
...CALM DOWN...
COLD!
OWW! OWW!
CALM...
...CALM...

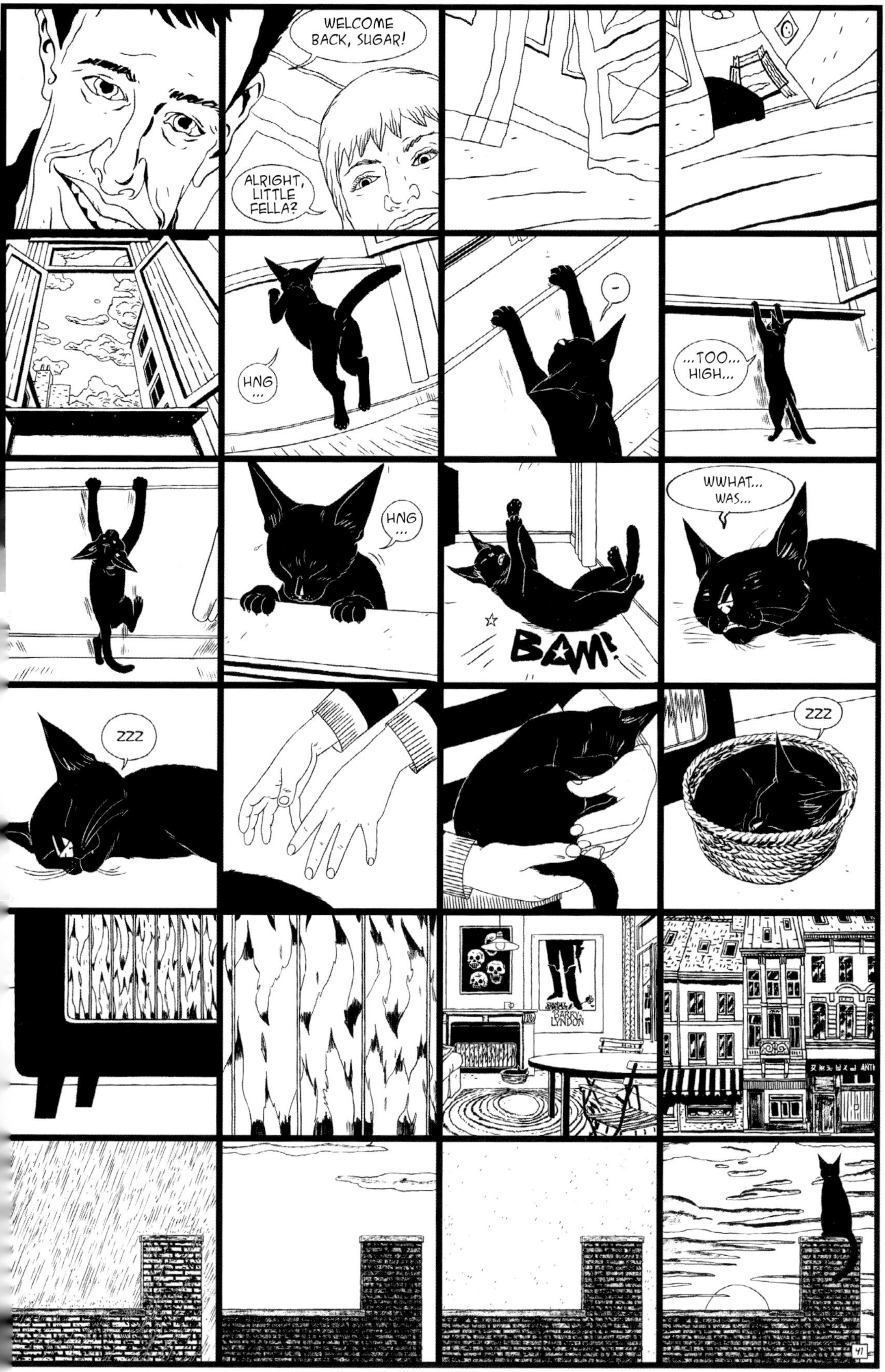
WELCOME BACK, SUGAR!
ALRIGHT, LITTLE FELLA?
HNG ...
...TOO... HIGH...
HNG ...
BAM!
WWHAT... WAS...
ZZZ
ZZZ
BARRY LYNDON

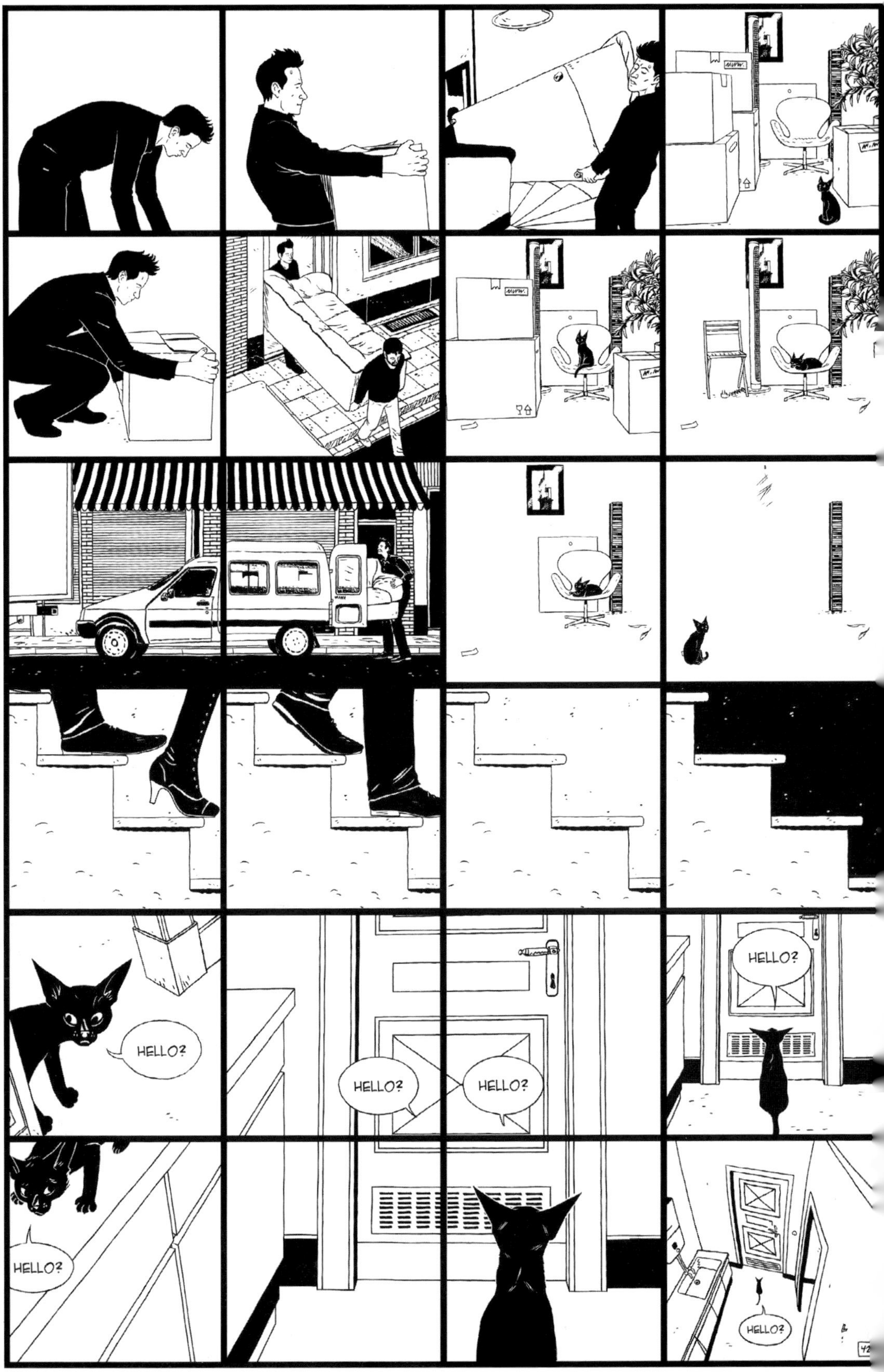
HELLO?
HELLO?
HELLO?
HELLO?
HELLO?
HELLO?

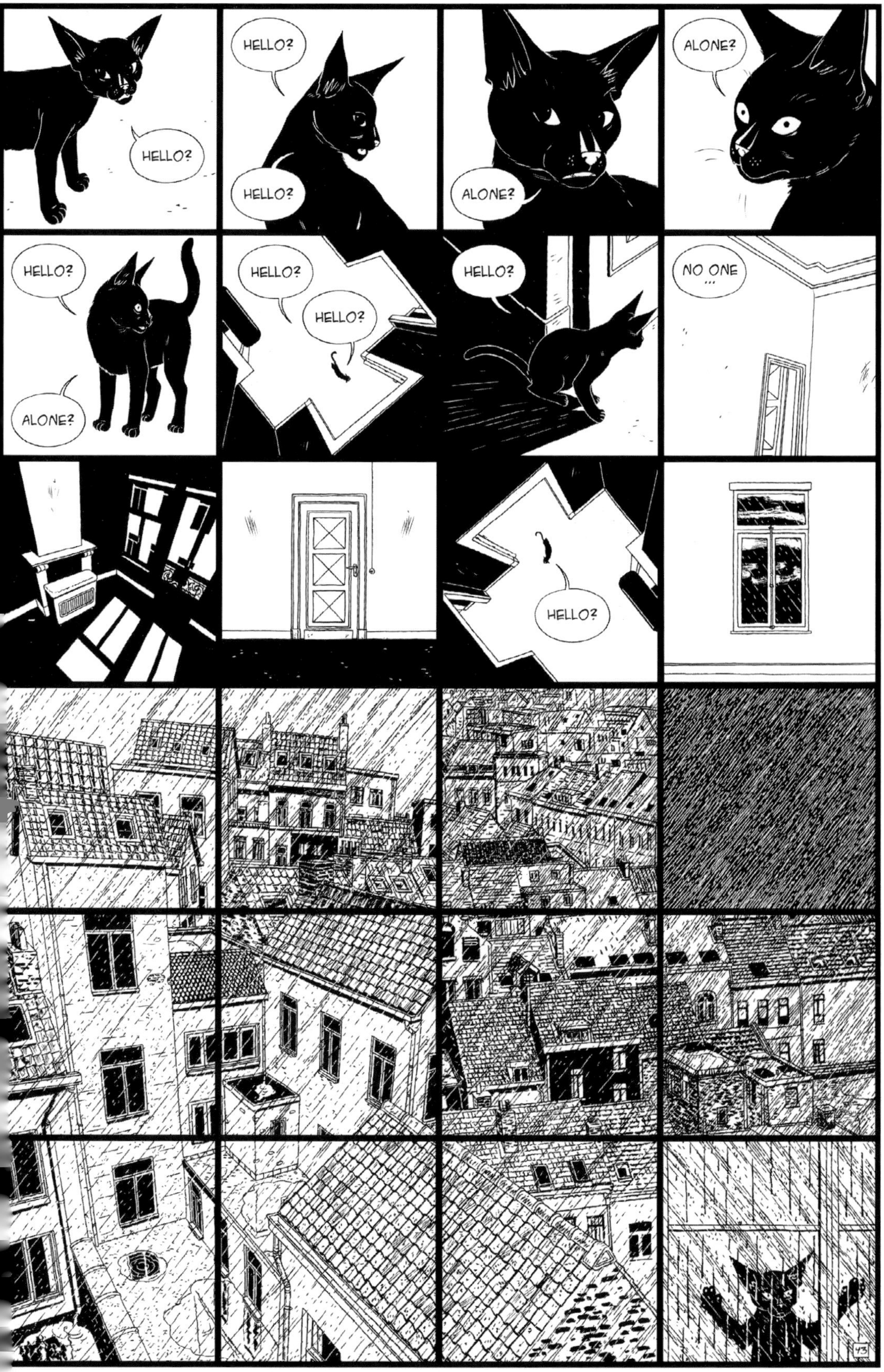
HELLO?
HELLO?
HELLO?
ALONE?
ALONE?
ALONE?
HELLO?
ALONE?
HELLO?
HELLO?
HELLO?
NO ONE ...
HELLO?
43

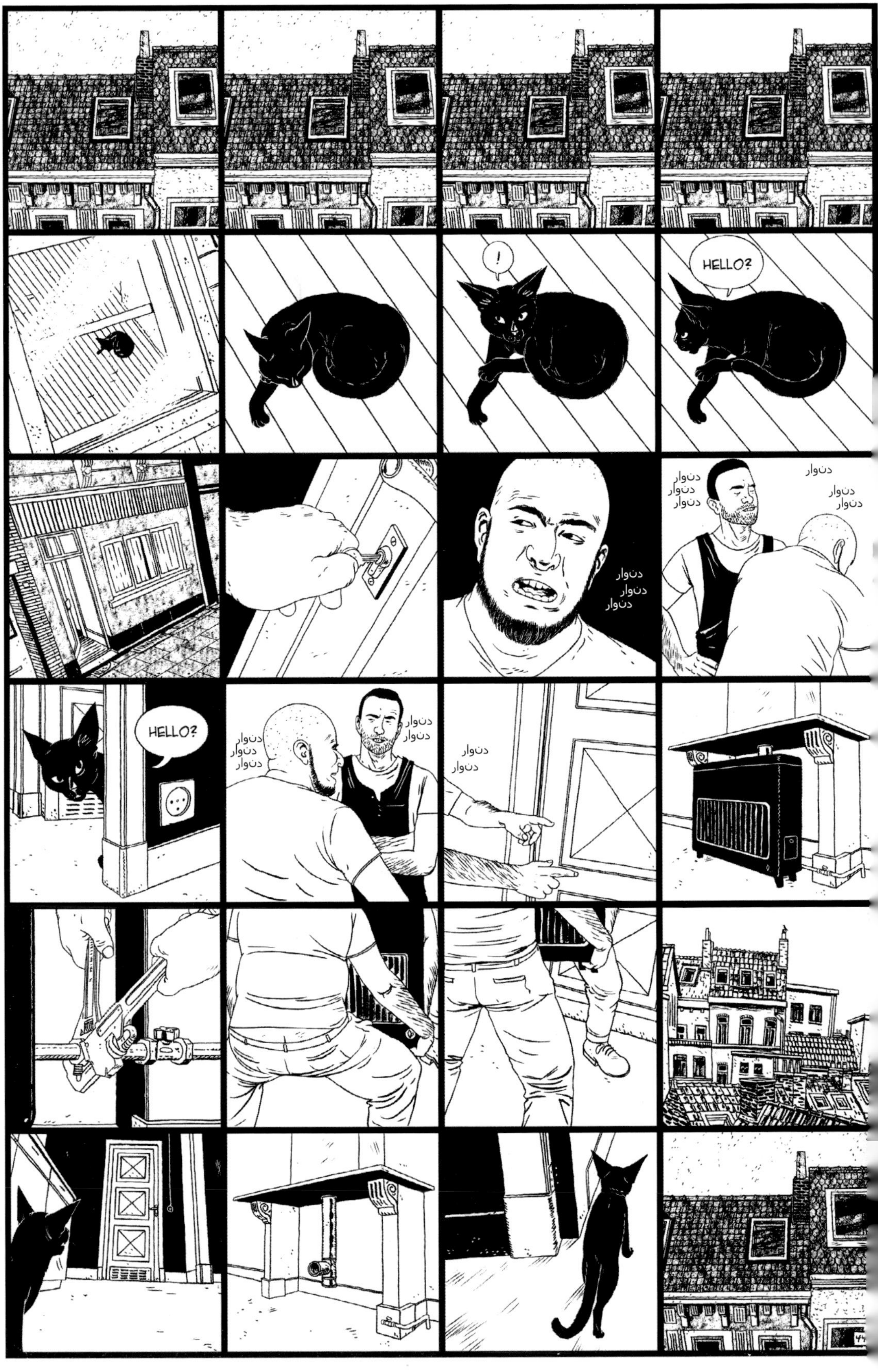
!
HELLO?
دنوار دنوار دنوار
دنوار دنوار دنوار
دنوار
دنوار دنوار
HELLO?
دنوار دنوار
دنوار دنوار دنوار
دنوار دنوار

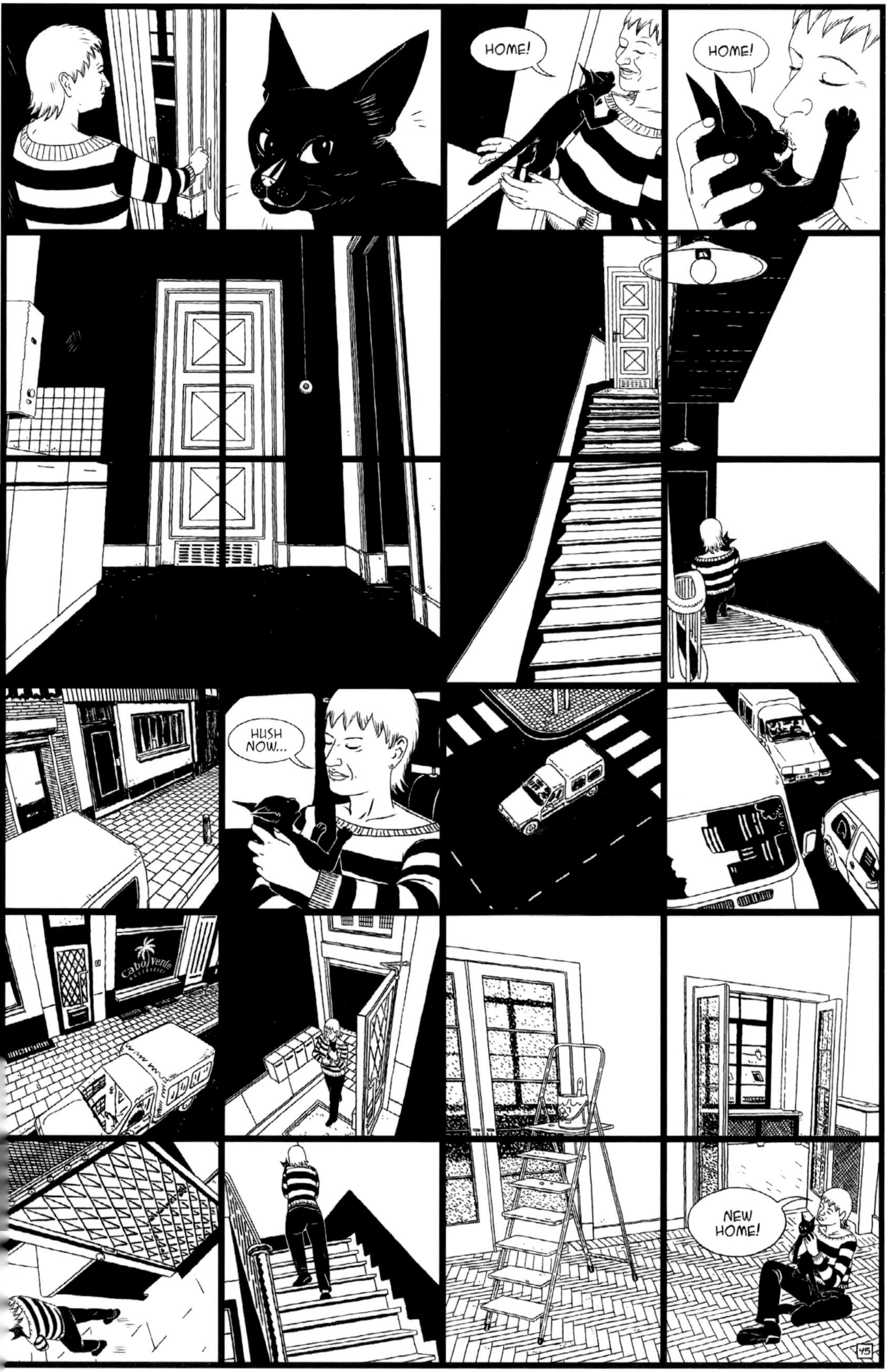

HOME!
HOME!
HUSH NOW...
Cabo Verde
NEW HOME!

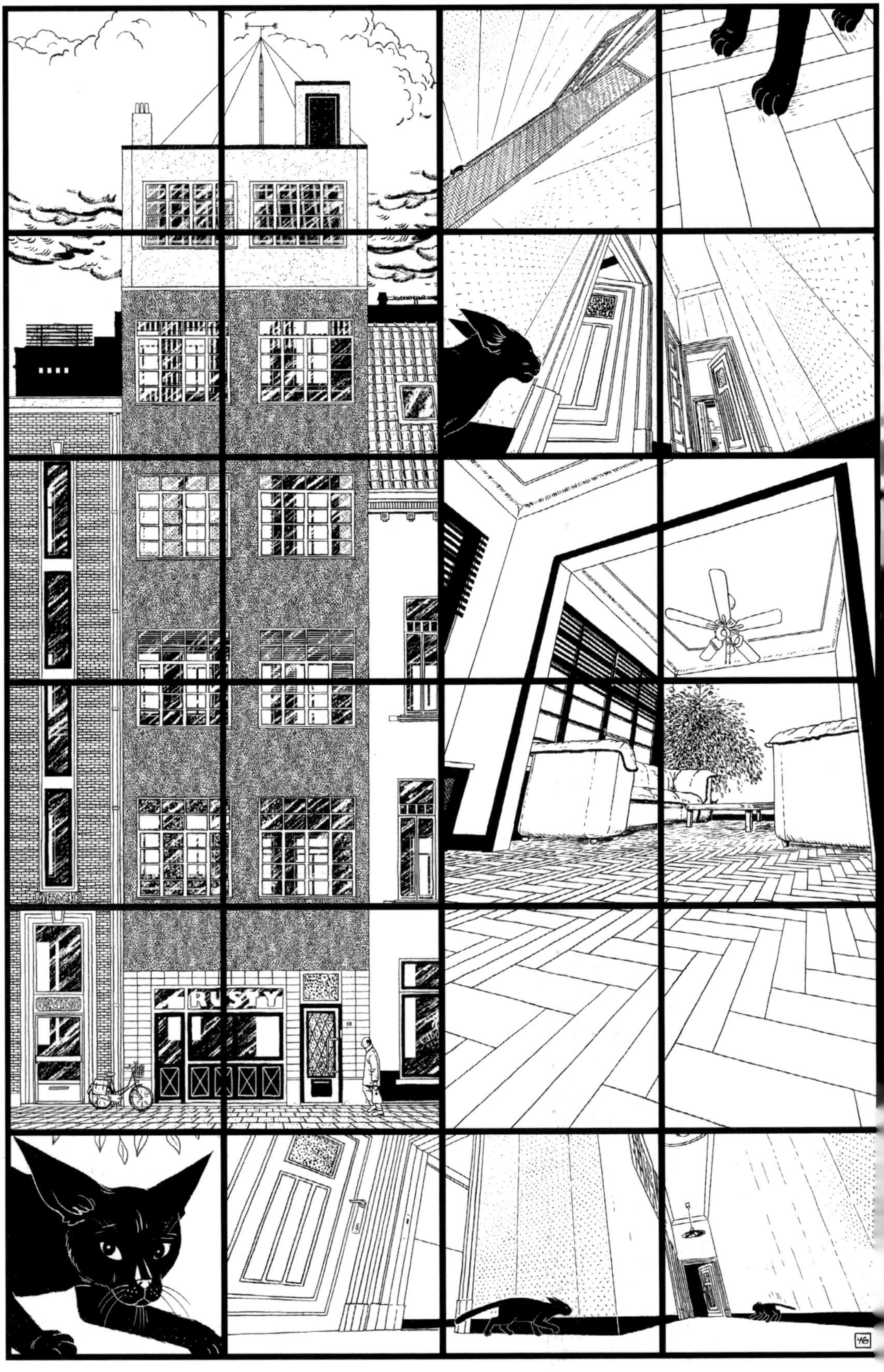
RUSTY

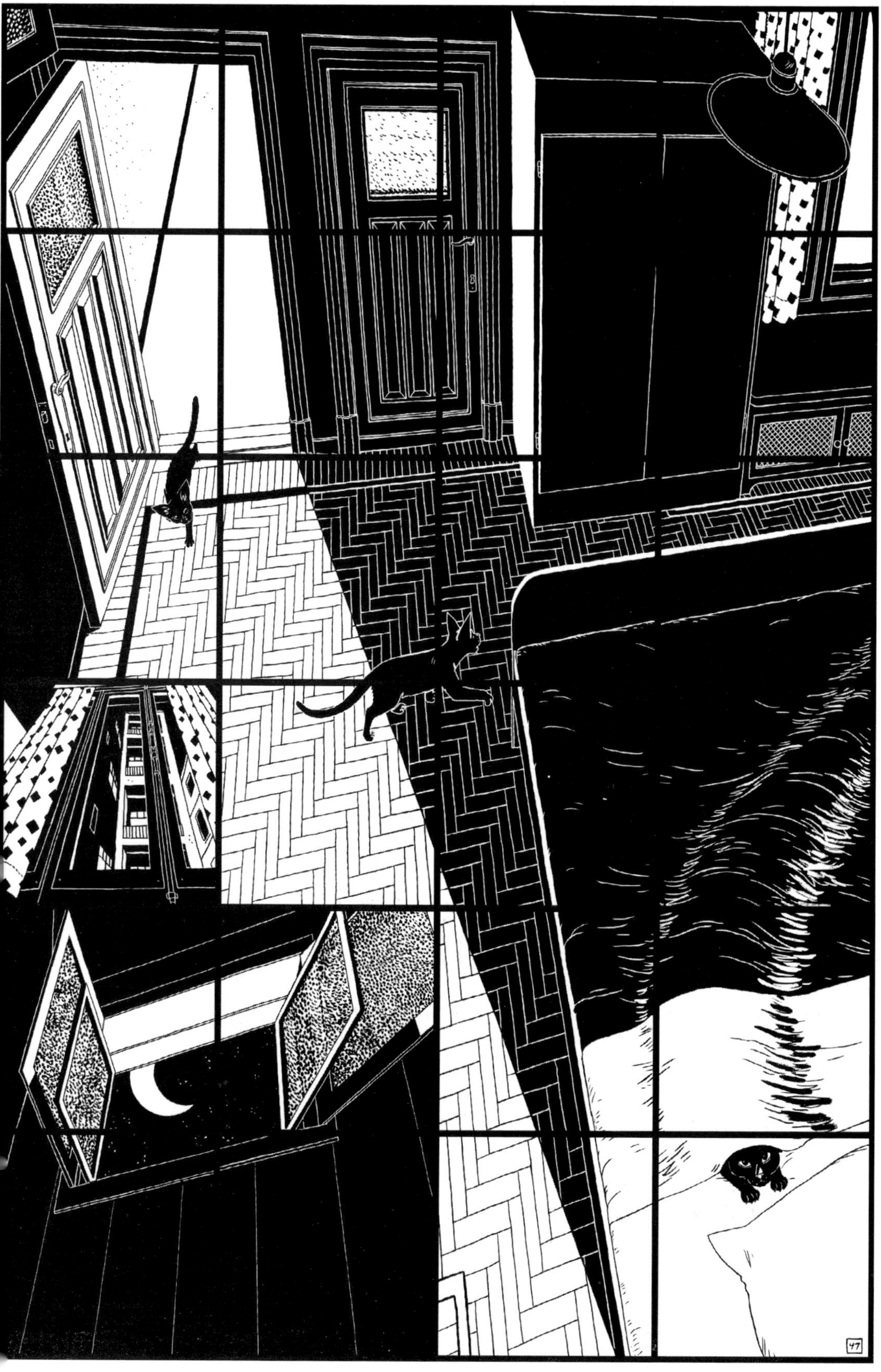

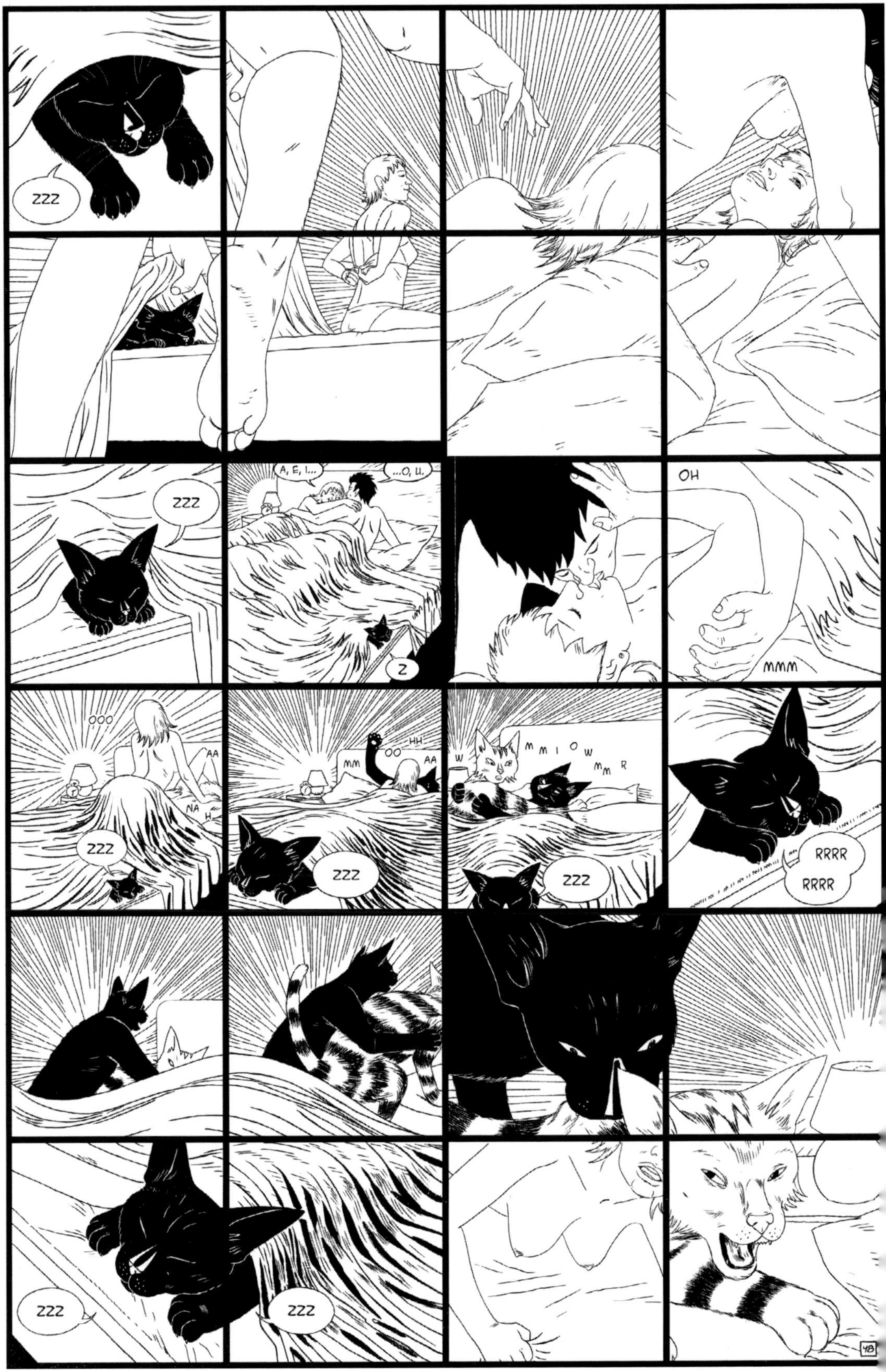
ZZZ
A, E, I...
...O, U.
Z
ZZZ
OH
MMM
OOO
AA
NA
H
ZZZ
OO
HH
MM
AA
ZZZ
W
M M I O W
M M R
ZZZ
RRRR
RRRR
ZZZ
ZZZ

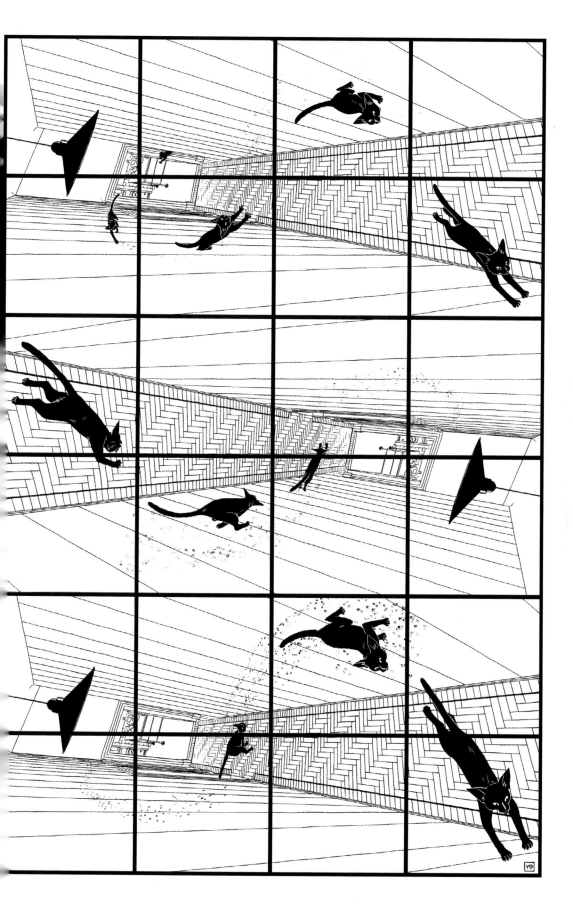

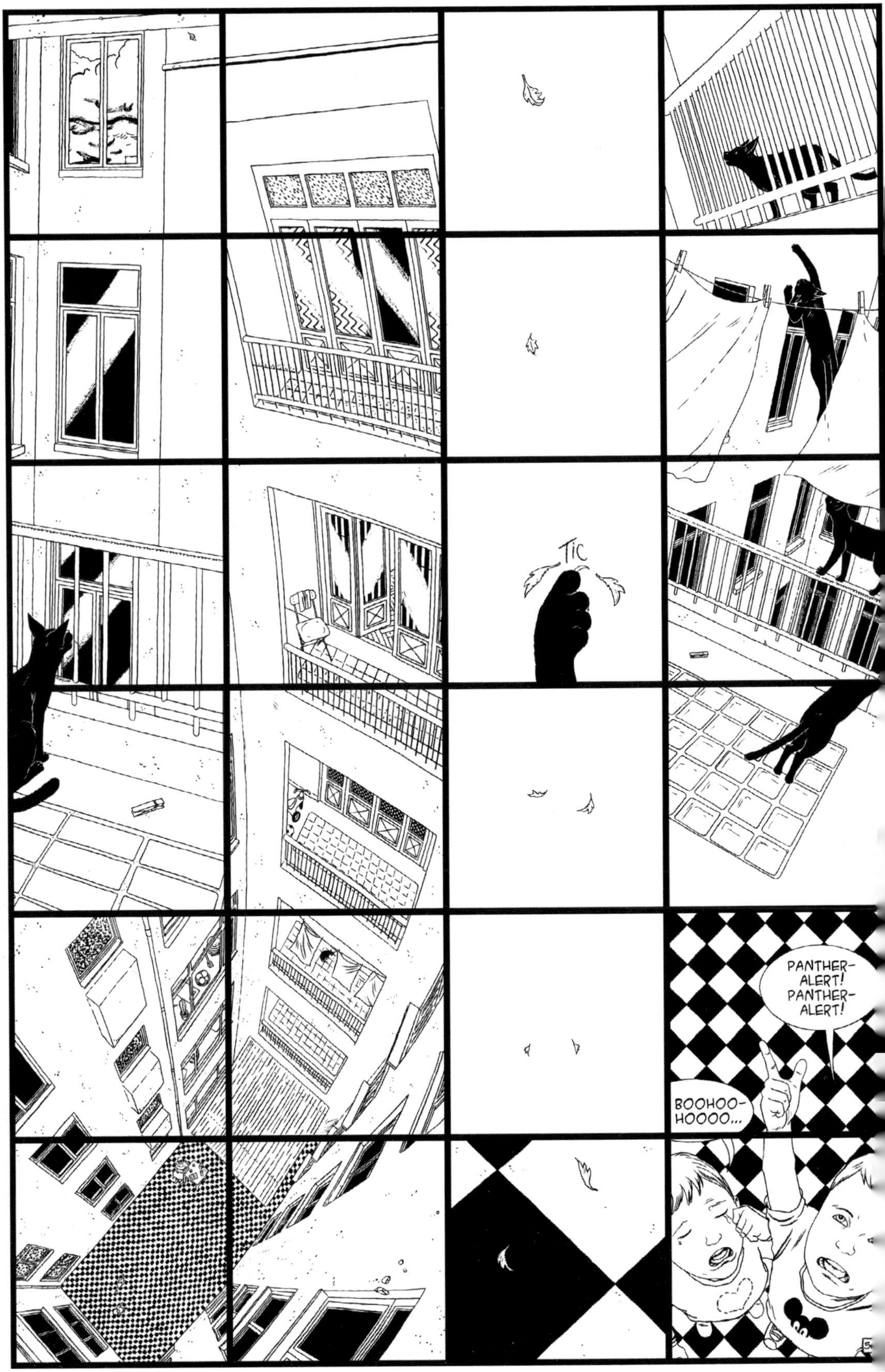
TIC
PANTHER-ALERT! PANTHER-ALERT!
BOOHOO-HOOOO...

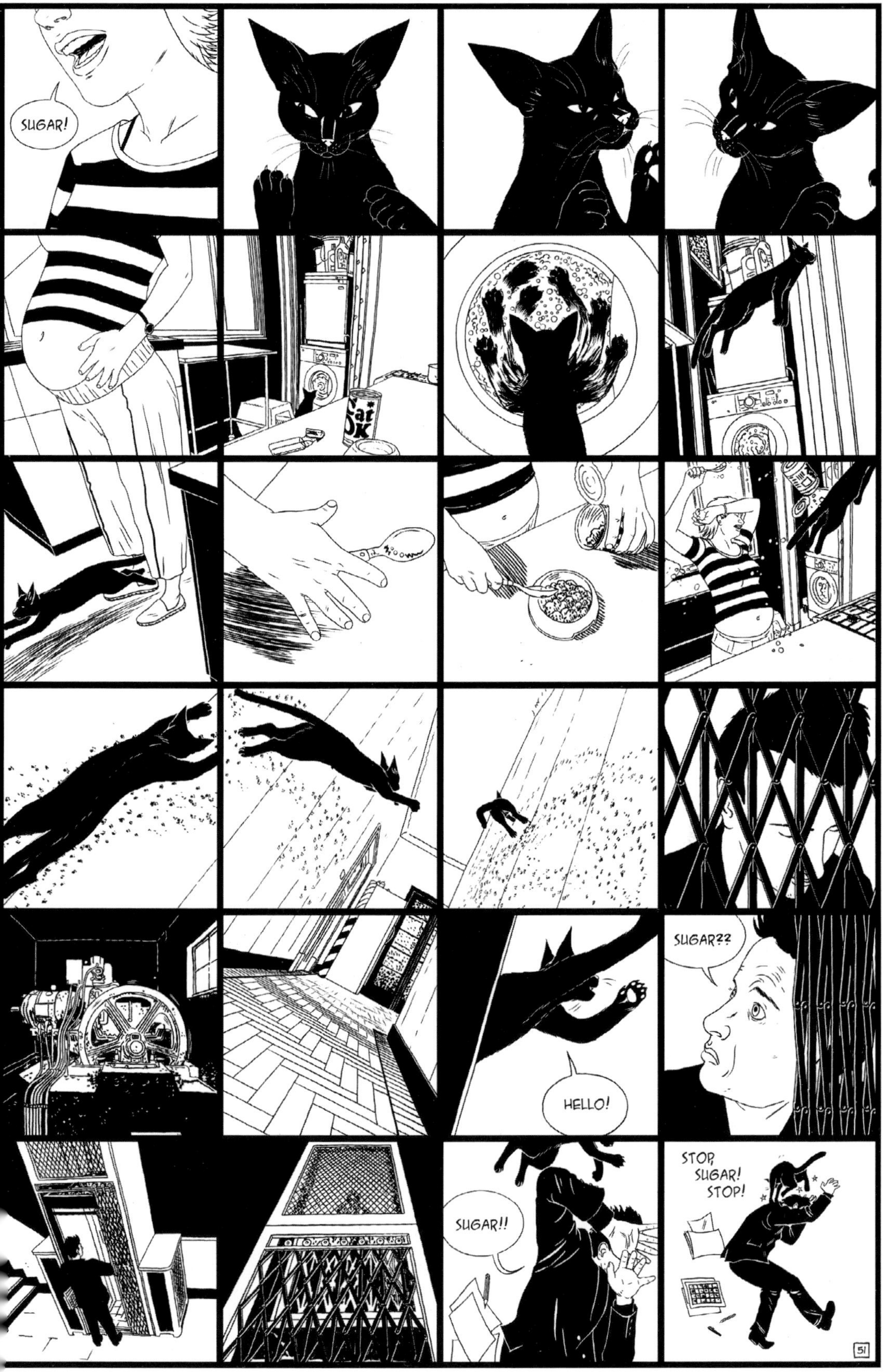
SUGAR!
SUGAR??
HELLO!
SUGAR!!
STOP, SUGAR! STOP!

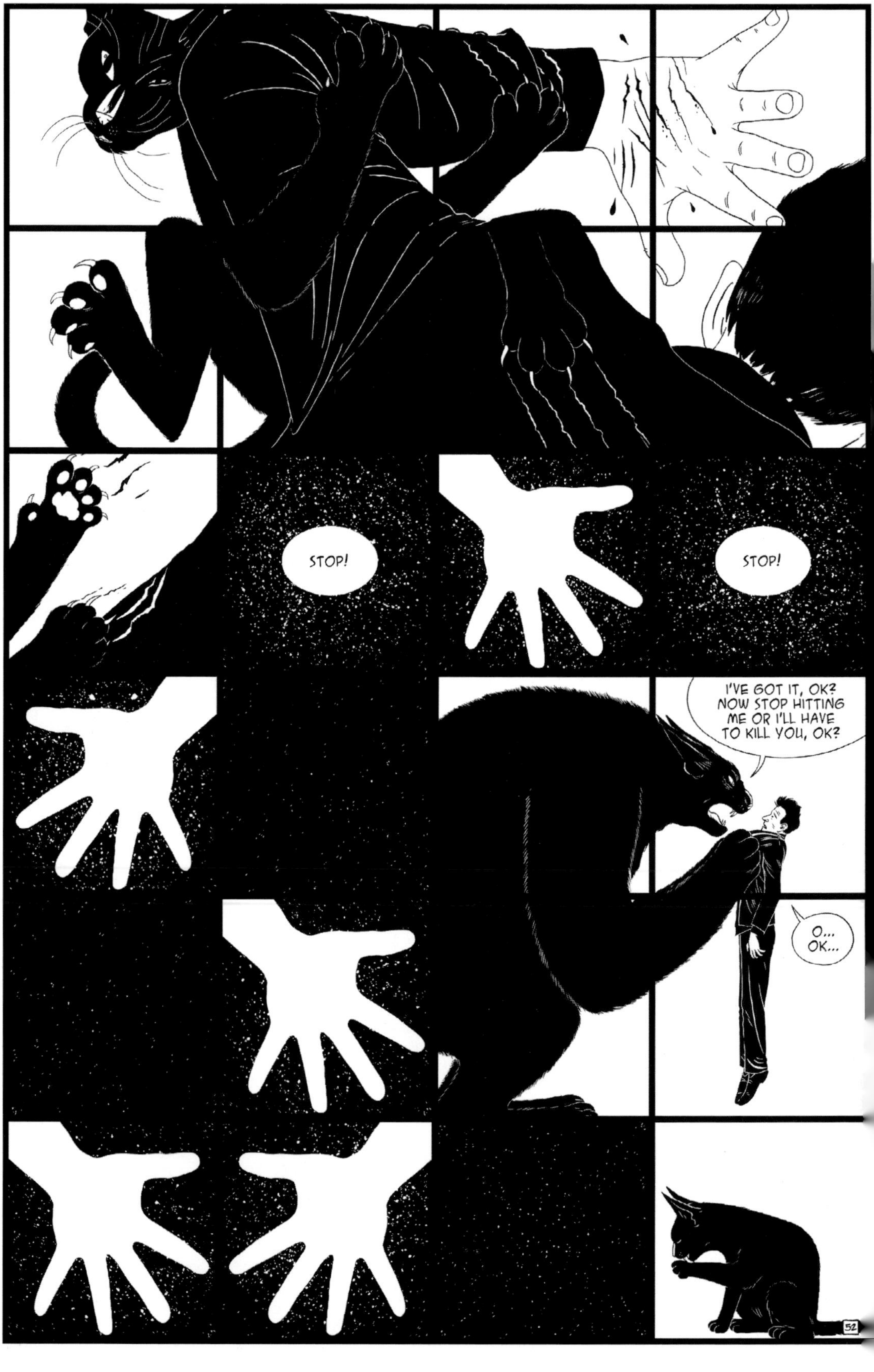
STOP!
STOP!
I'VE GOT IT, OK?
NOW STOP HITTING
ME OR I'LL HAVE
TO KILL YOU, OK?
O...
OK...

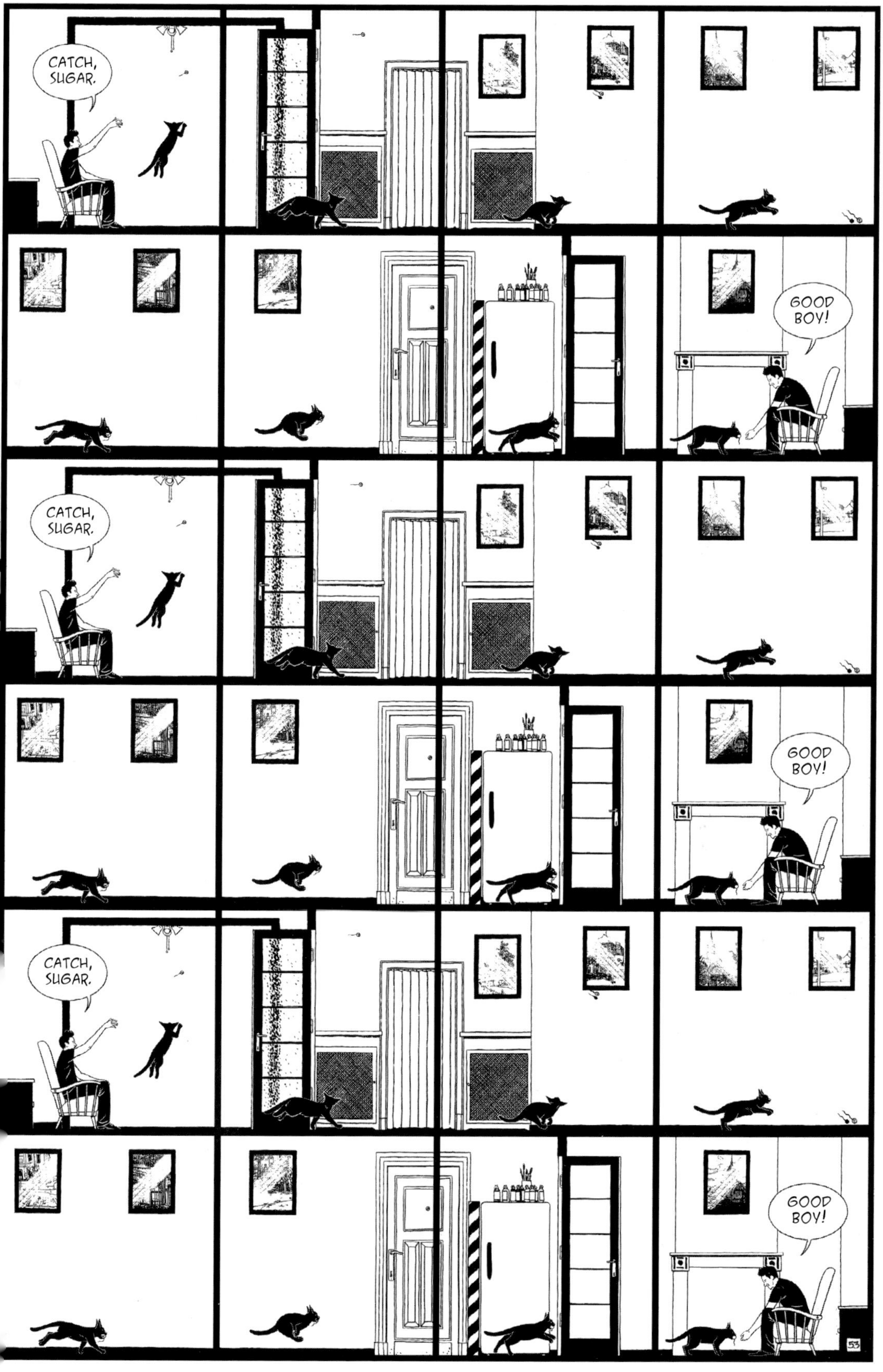
CATCH, SUGAR.
GOOD BOY!
CATCH, SUGAR.
GOOD BOY!
CATCH, SUGAR.
GOOD BOY!
53

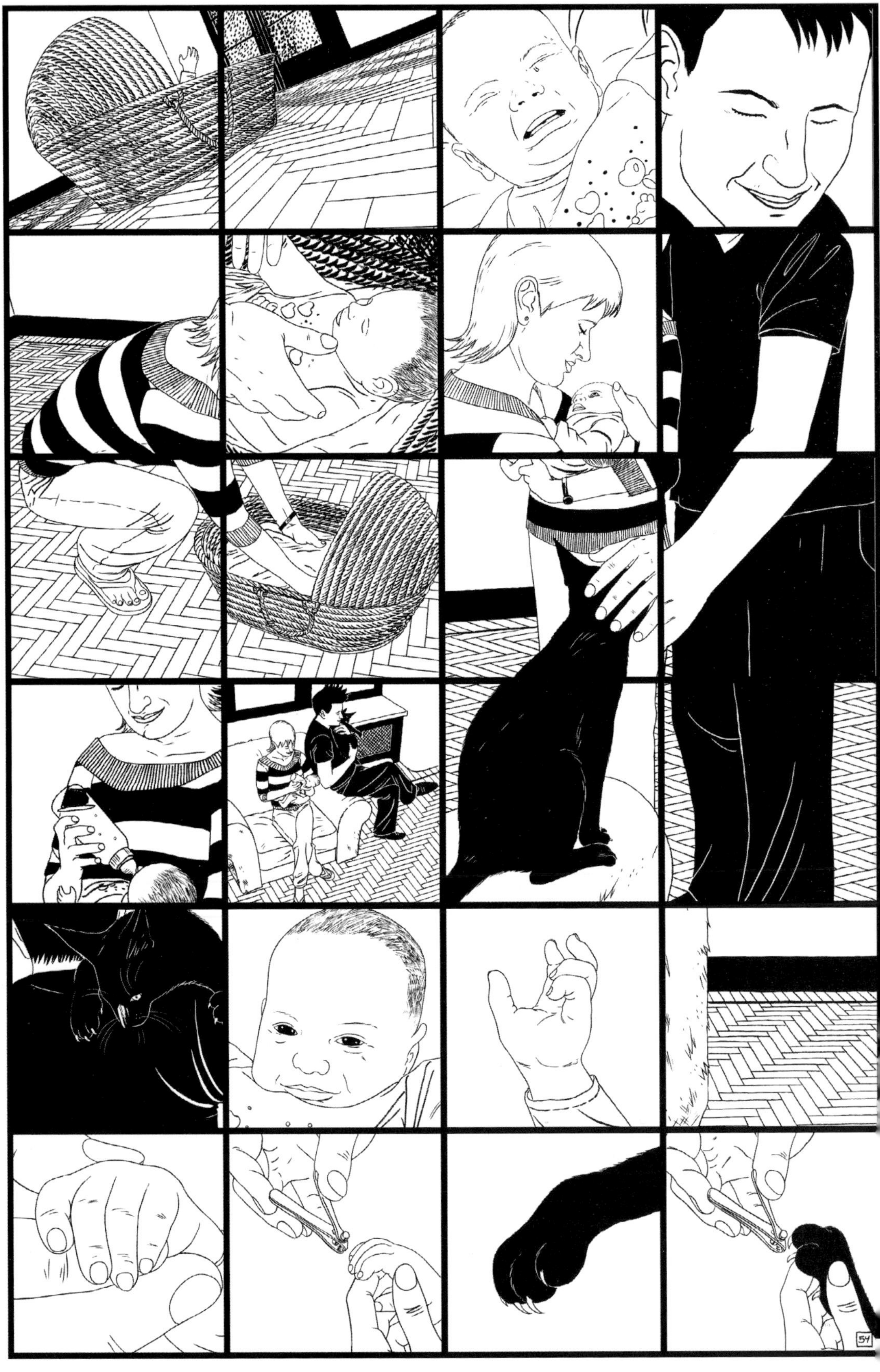

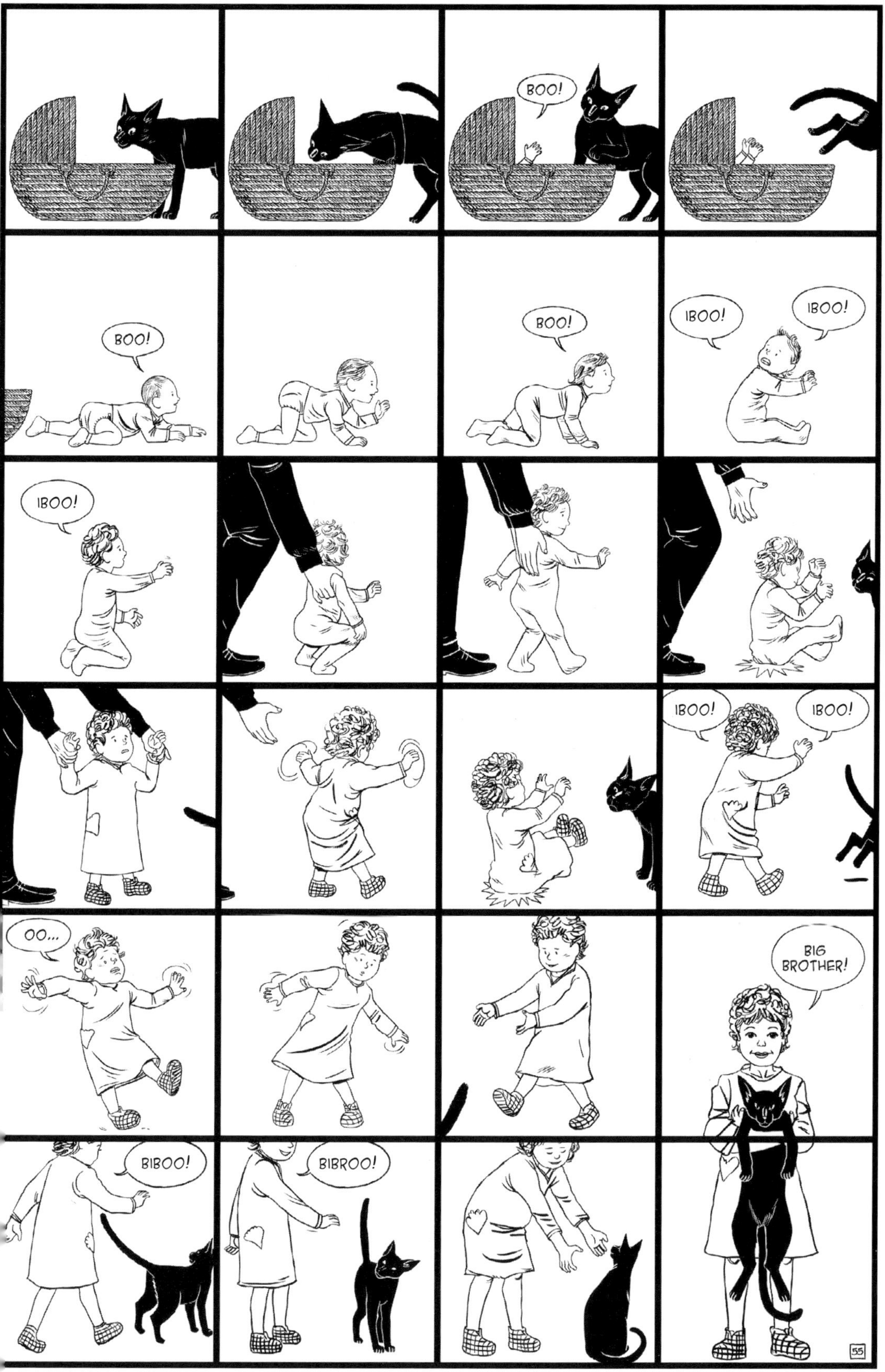
BOO!
BOO!
BOO!
IBOO!
IBOO!
IBOO!
IBOO!
IBOO!
OO...
BIG BROTHER!
BIBOO!
BIBROO!

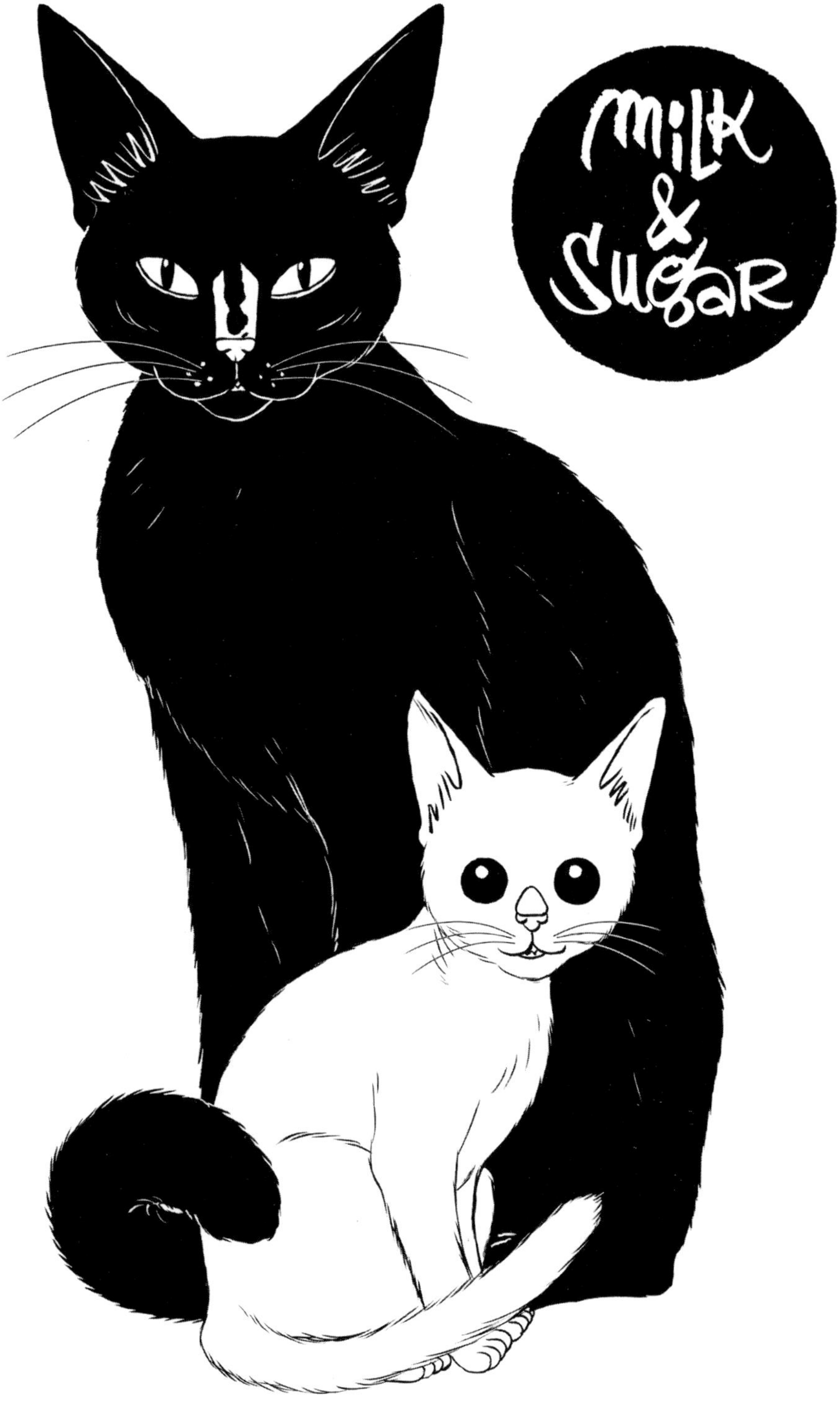
Milk
&
Sugar

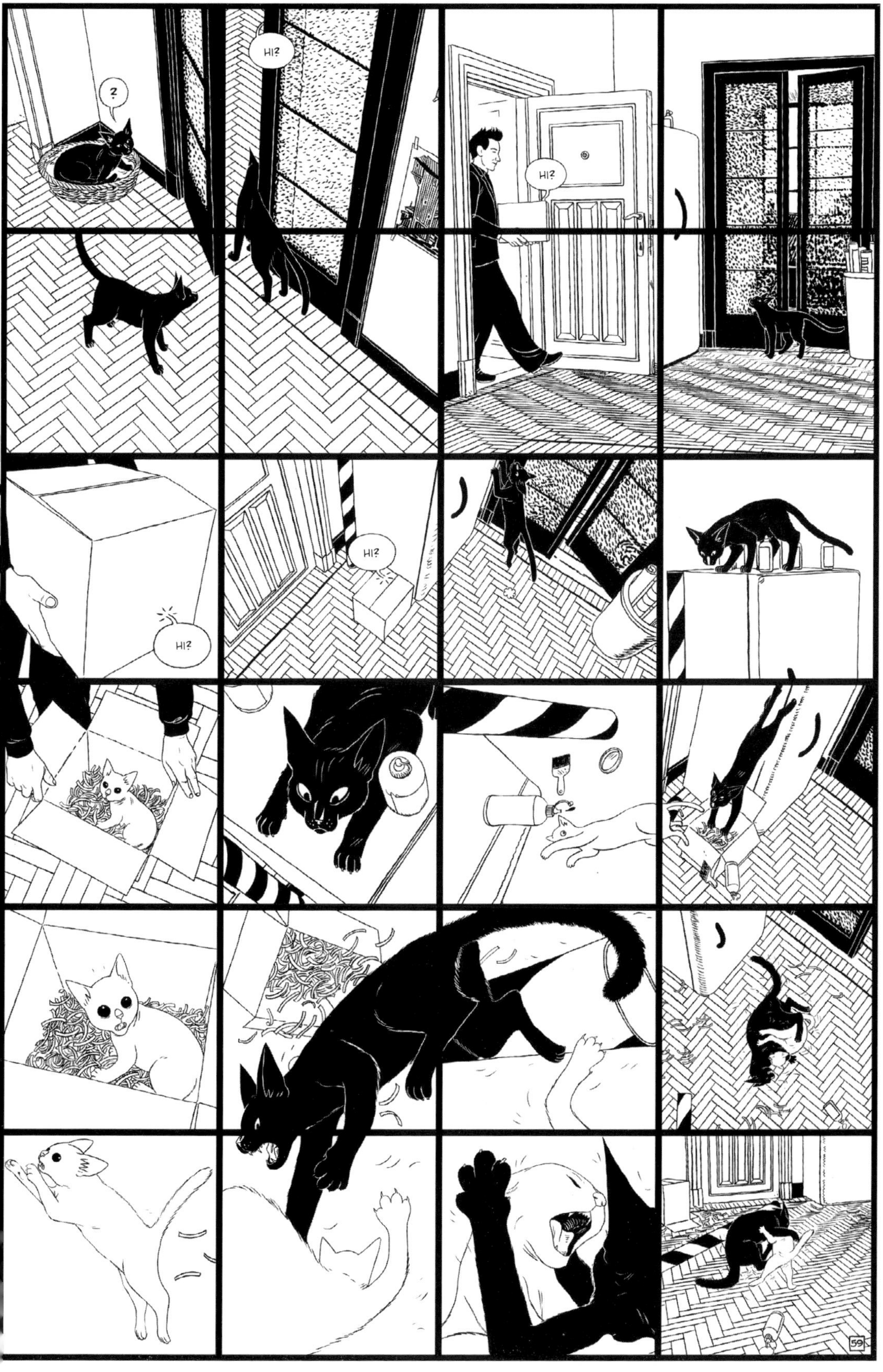
?
HI?
HI?
HI?
HI?

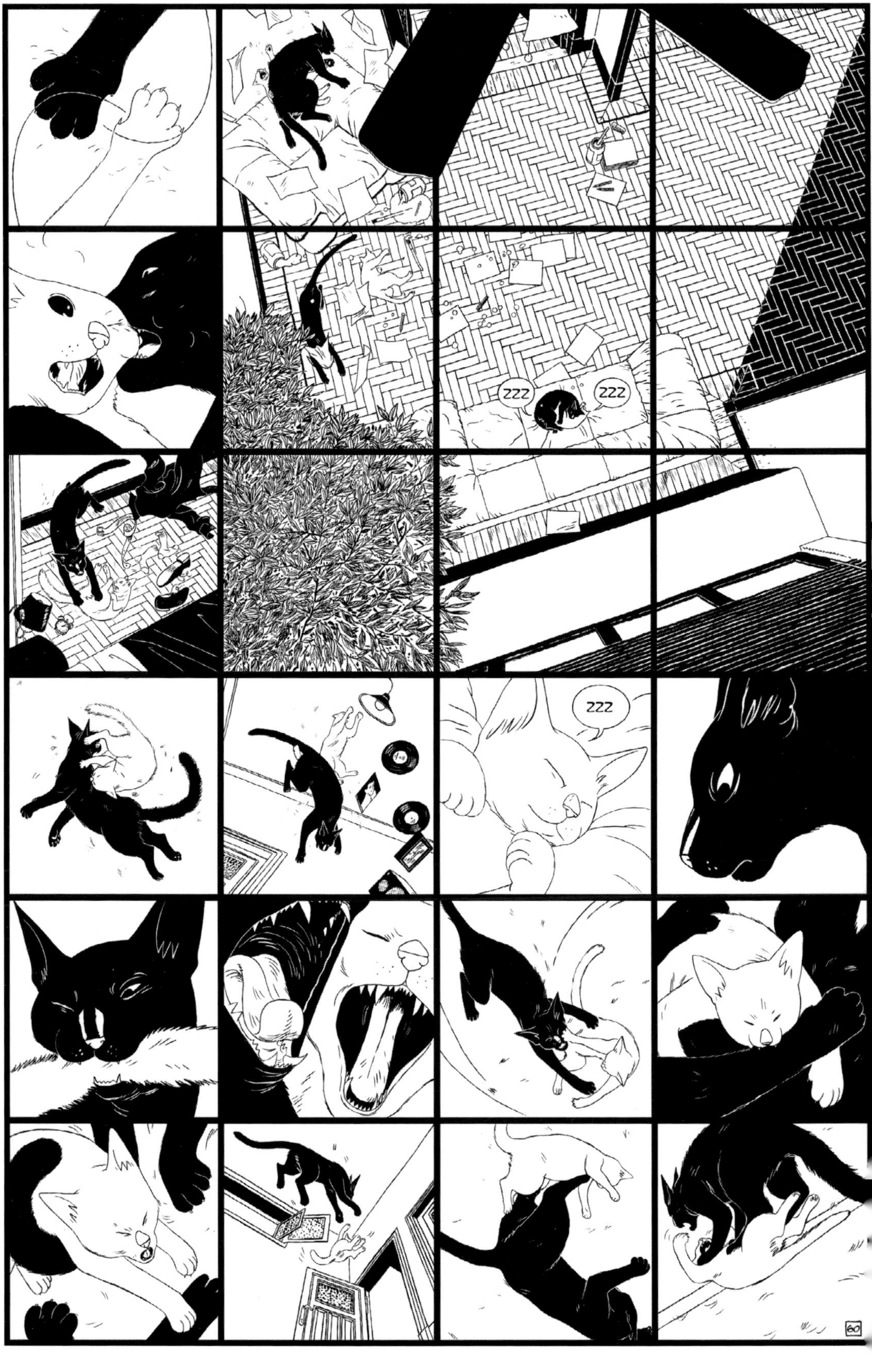
ZZZ
ZZZ
ZZZ

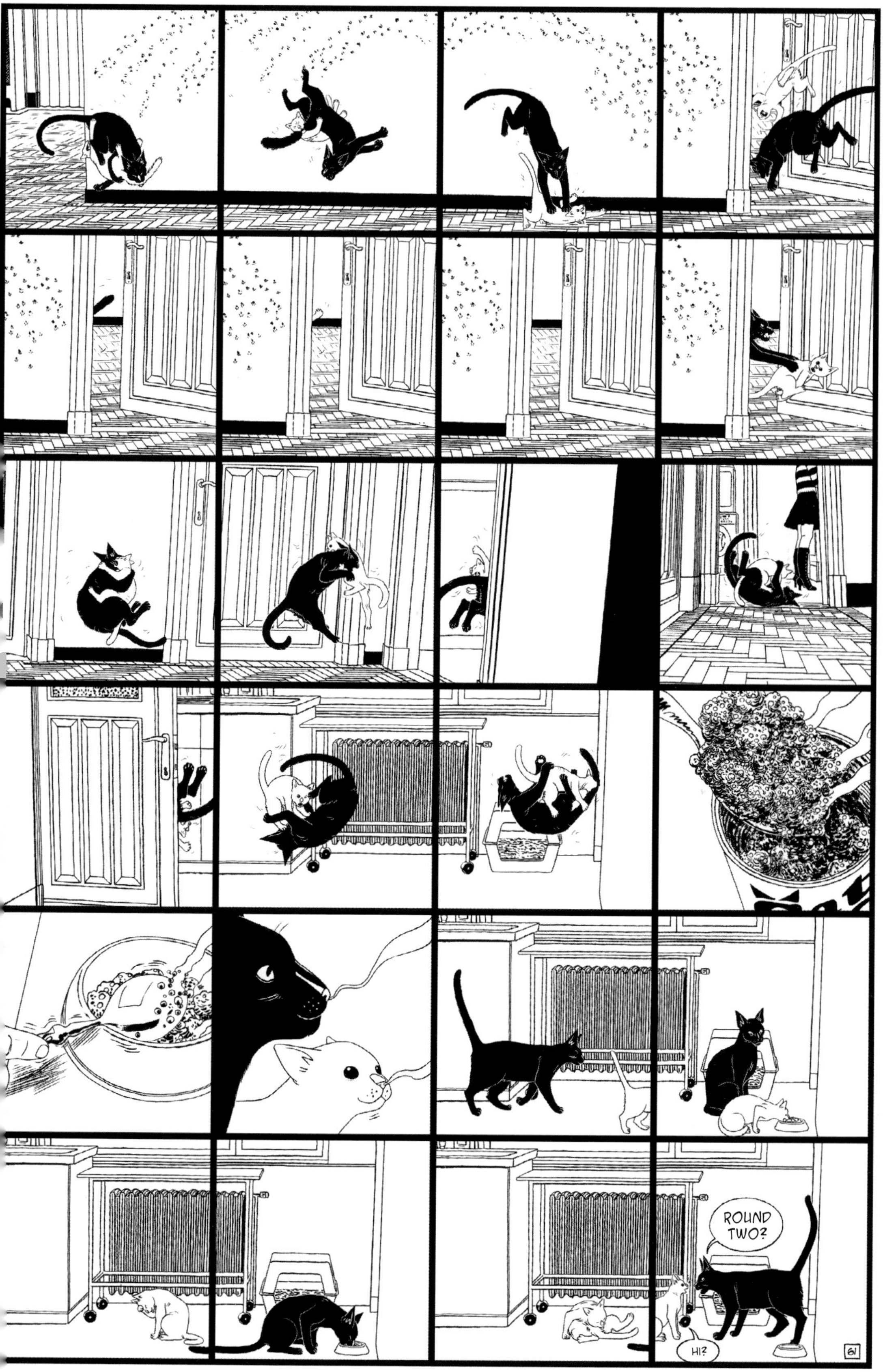
ROUND TWO?
HI?
61

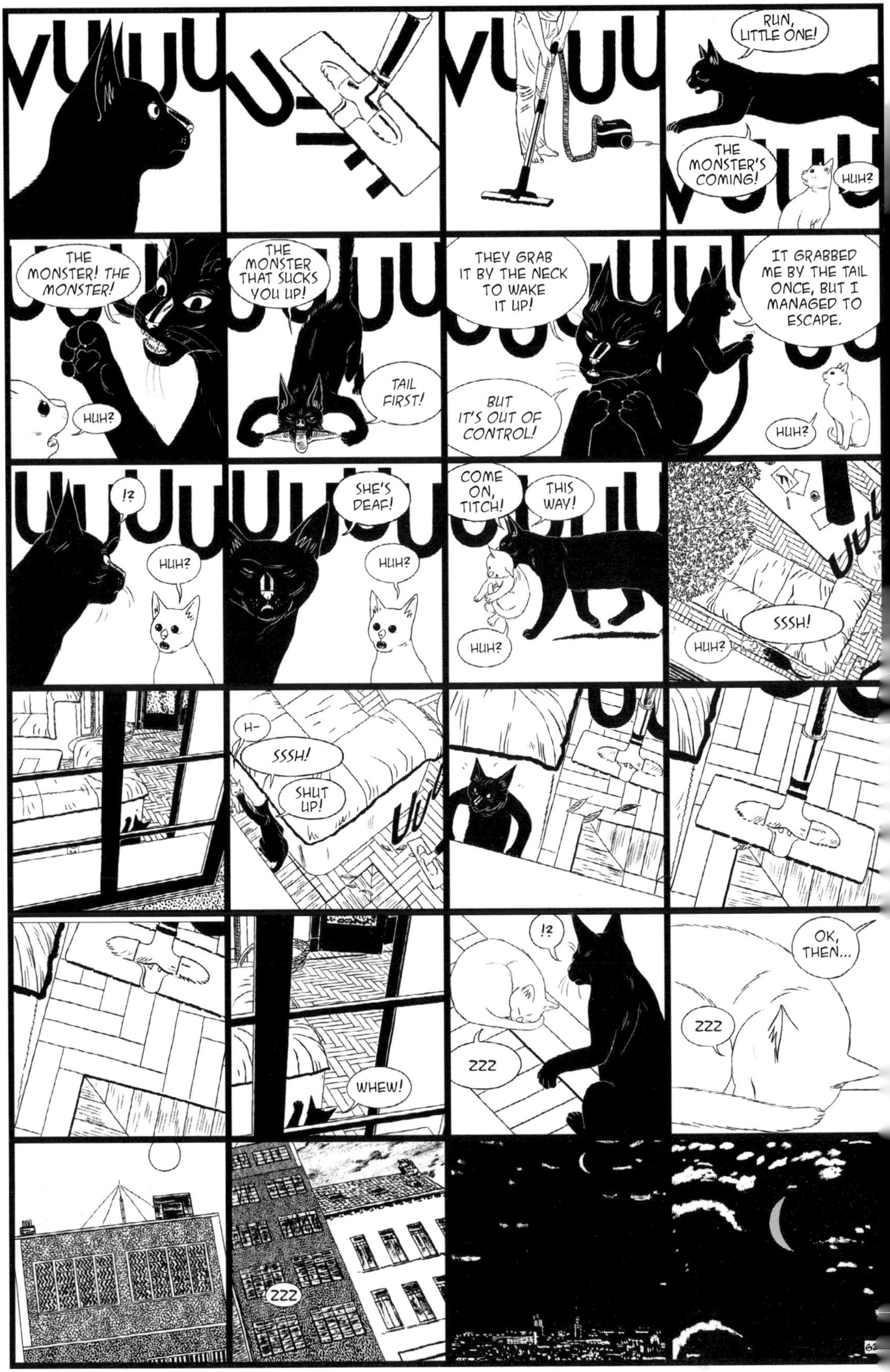
RUN, LITTLE ONE!
THE MONSTER'S COMING!
HUH?
THE MONSTER! THE MONSTER!
HUH?
THE MONSTER THAT SUCKS YOU UP!
TAIL FIRST!
THEY GRAB IT BY THE NECK TO WAKE IT UP!
BUT IT'S OUT OF CONTROL!
IT GRABBED ME BY THE TAIL ONCE, BUT I MANAGED TO ESCAPE.
HUH?
!?
HUH?
SHE'S DEAF!
HUH?
COME ON, TITCH!
THIS WAY!
HUH?
SSSH!
HUH?
H-
SSSH!
SHUT UP!
WHEW!
!?
ZZZ
OK, THEN...
ZZZ
ZZZ

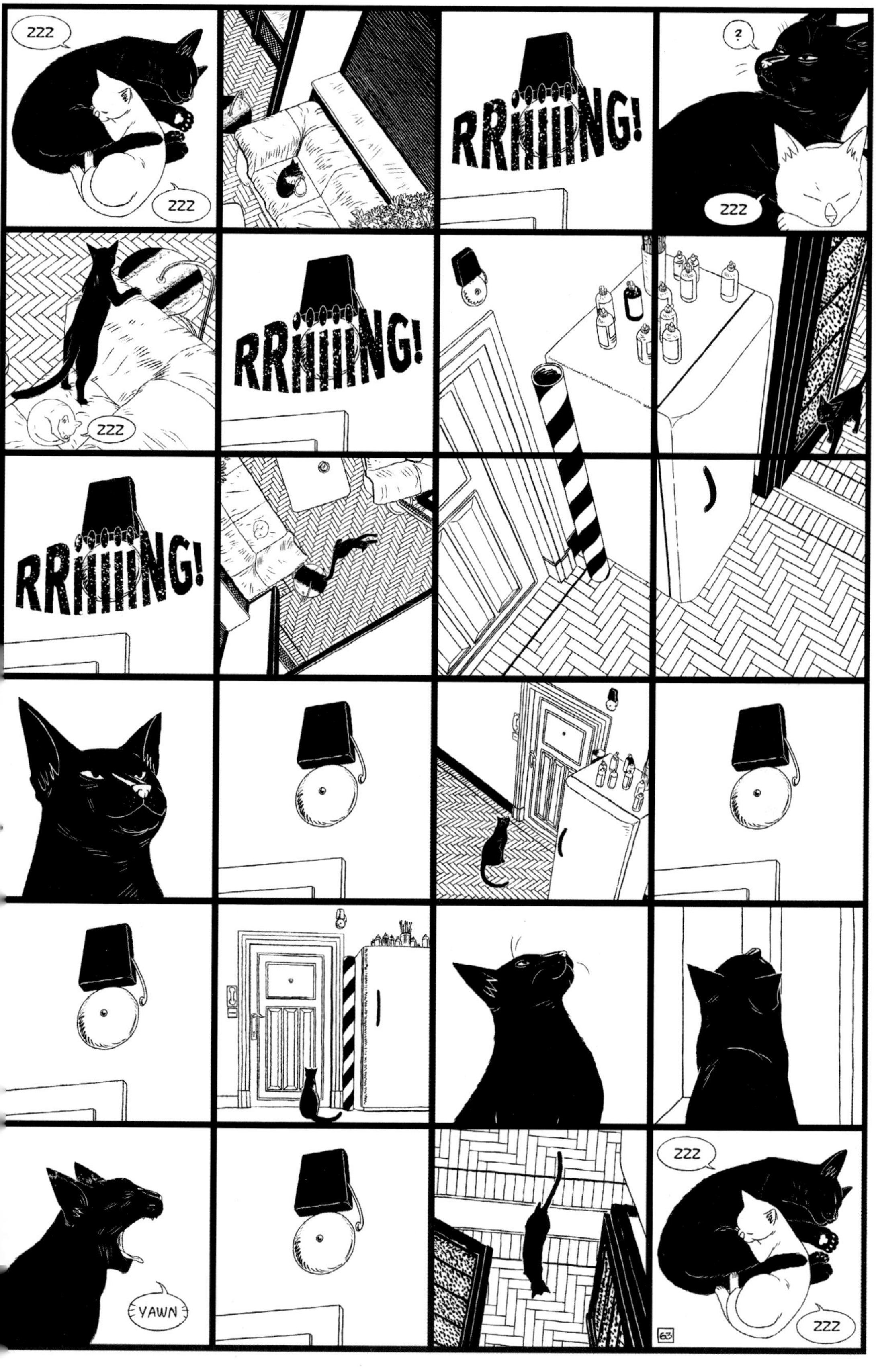
ZZZ
ZZZ
RRHIIING!
?
ZZZ
ZZZ
RRHIIING!
RRHIIING!
YAWN
ZZZ
ZZZ

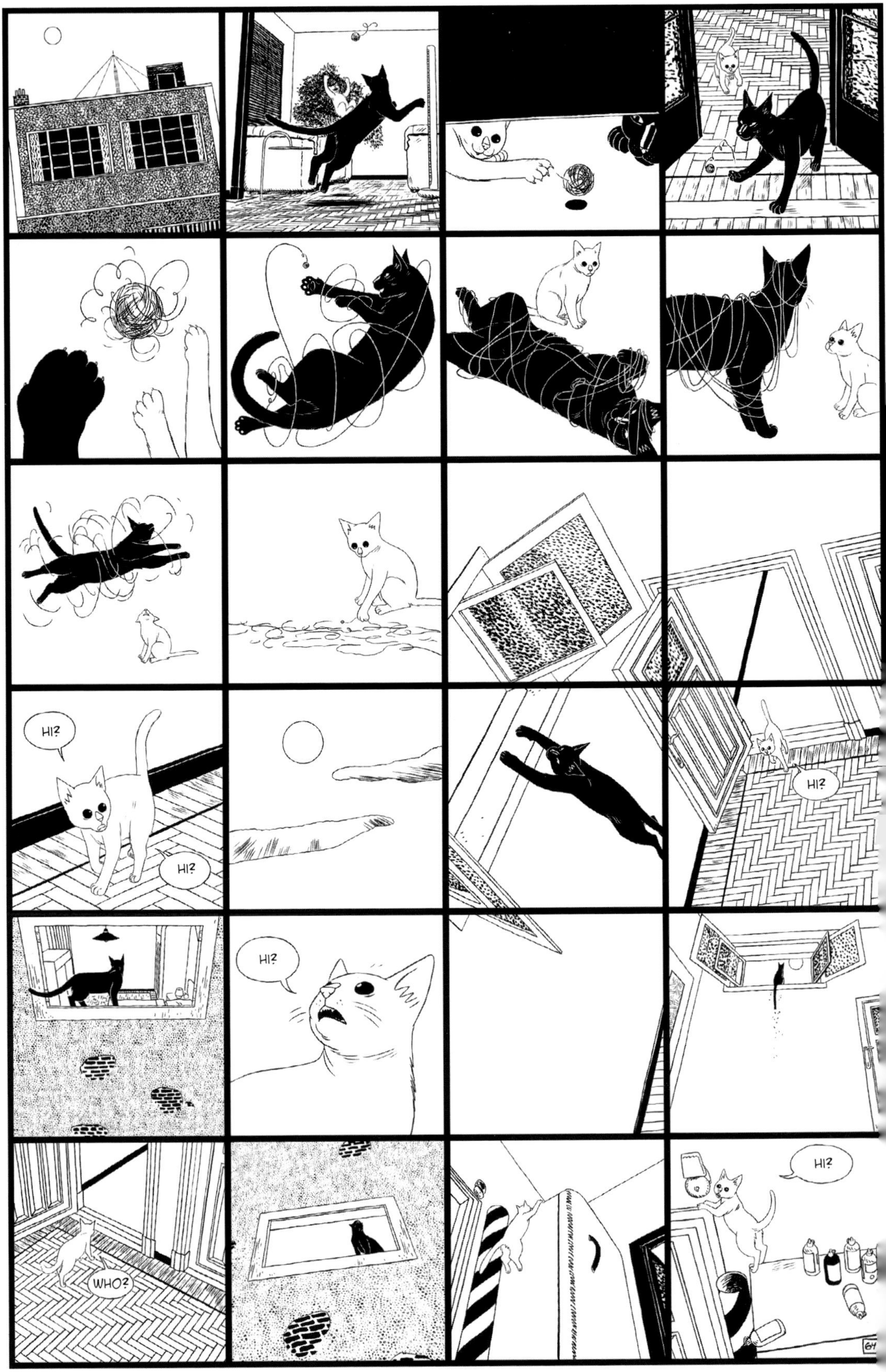
HI?
HI?
HI?
HI?
WHO?
HI?

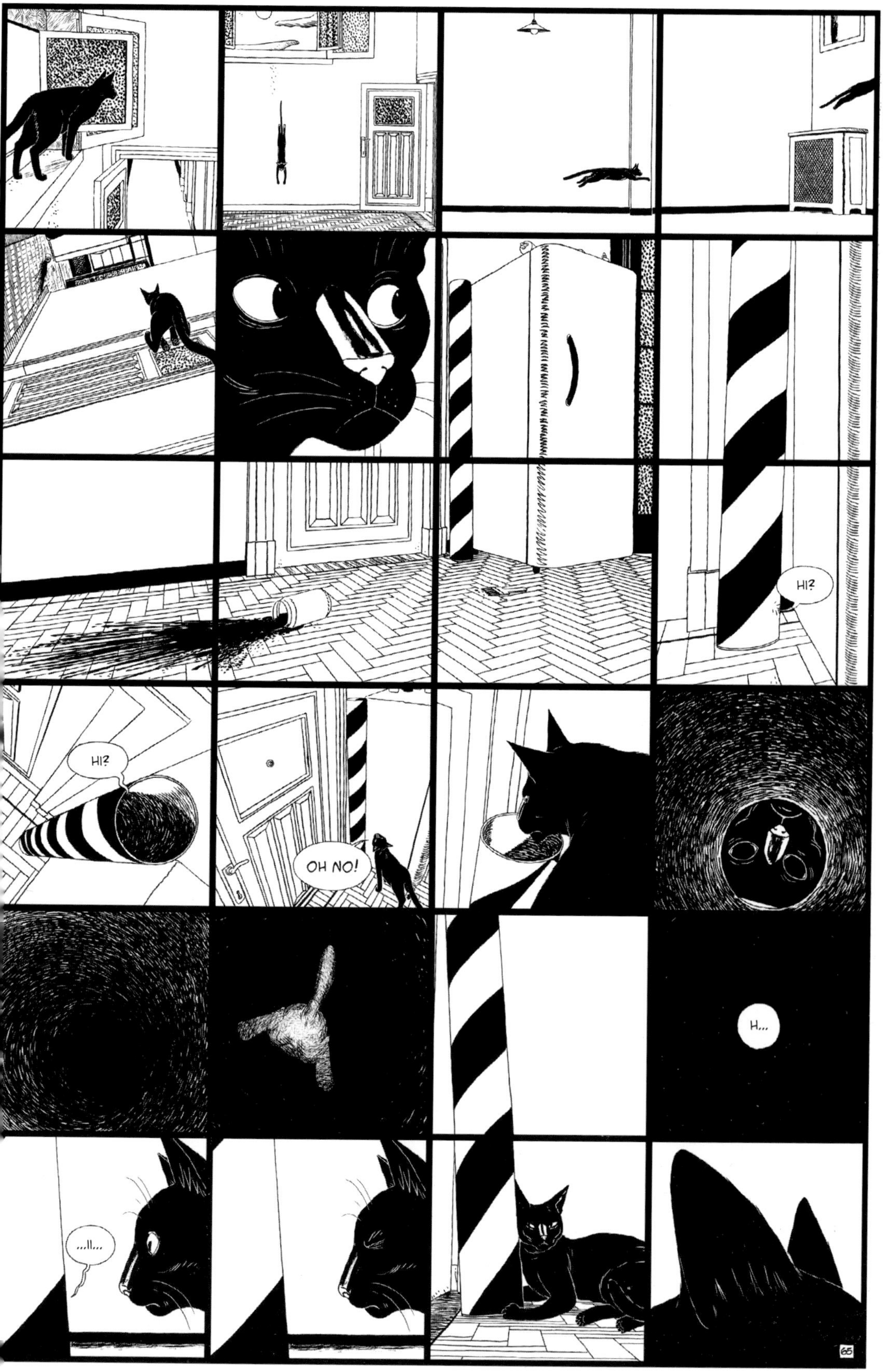
HI?
HI?
OH NO!
H...
...I...

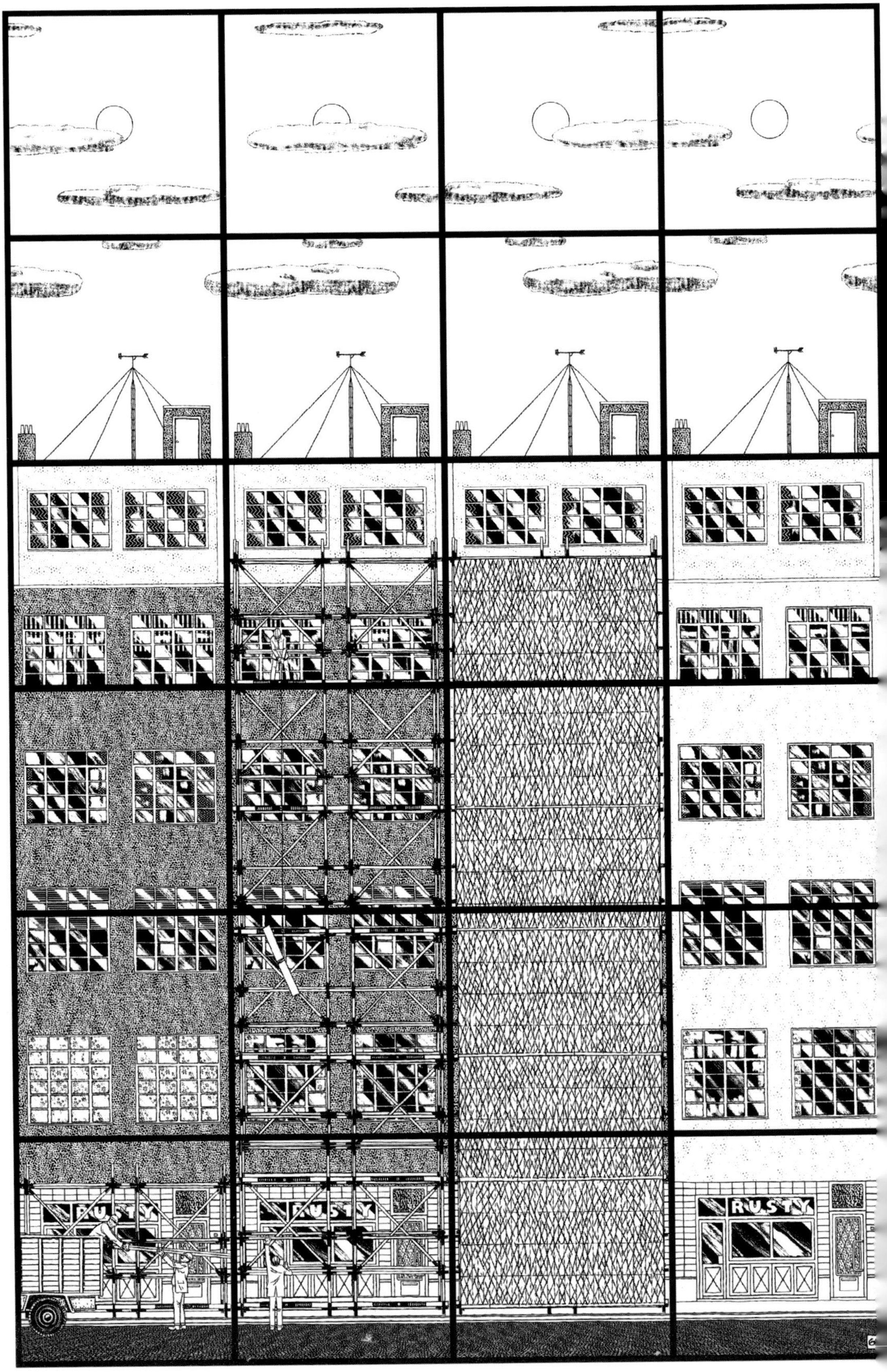
RUSTY
RUSTY
RUSTY

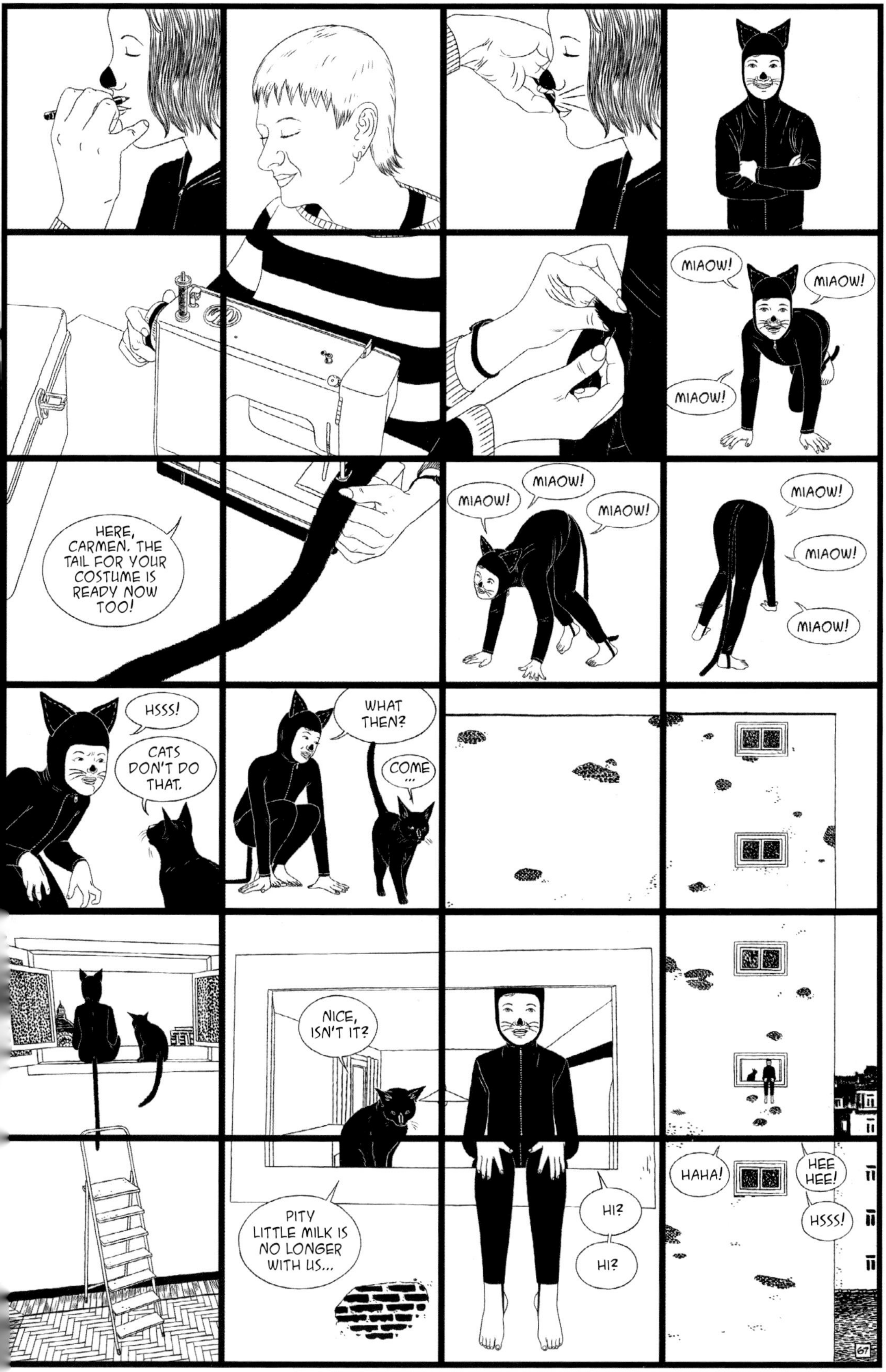
MIAOW!
MIAOW!
MIAOW!
HERE, CARMEN. THE TAIL FOR YOUR COSTUME IS READY NOW TOO!
MIAOW!
MIAOW!
MIAOW!
MIAOW!
MIAOW!
MIAOW!
HSSS!
CATS DON'T DO THAT.
WHAT THEN?
COME ...
NICE, ISN'T IT?
PITY LITTLE MILK IS NO LONGER WITH US...
HI?
HI?
HAHA!
HEE HEE!
HSSS!

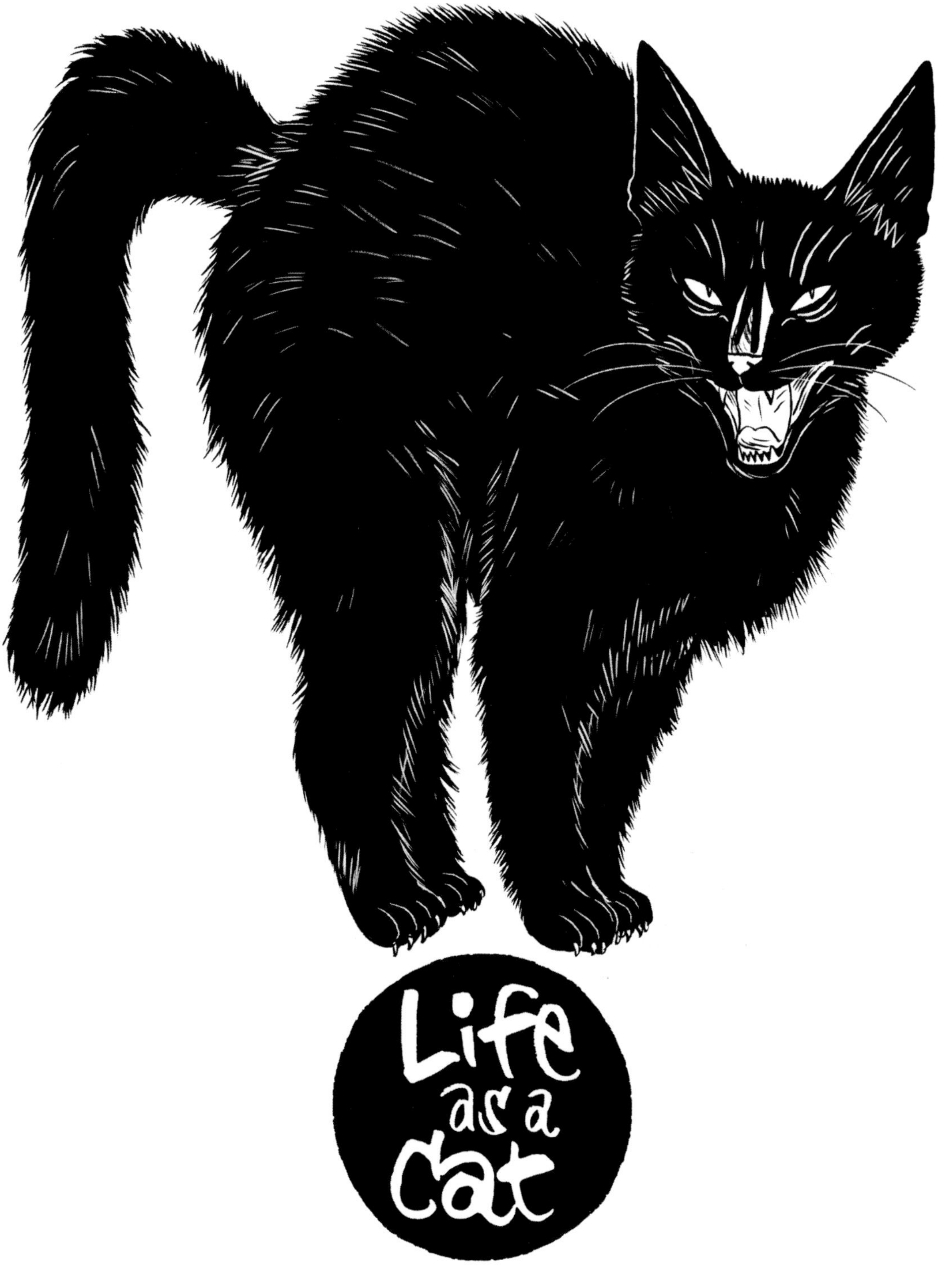
Life as a cat

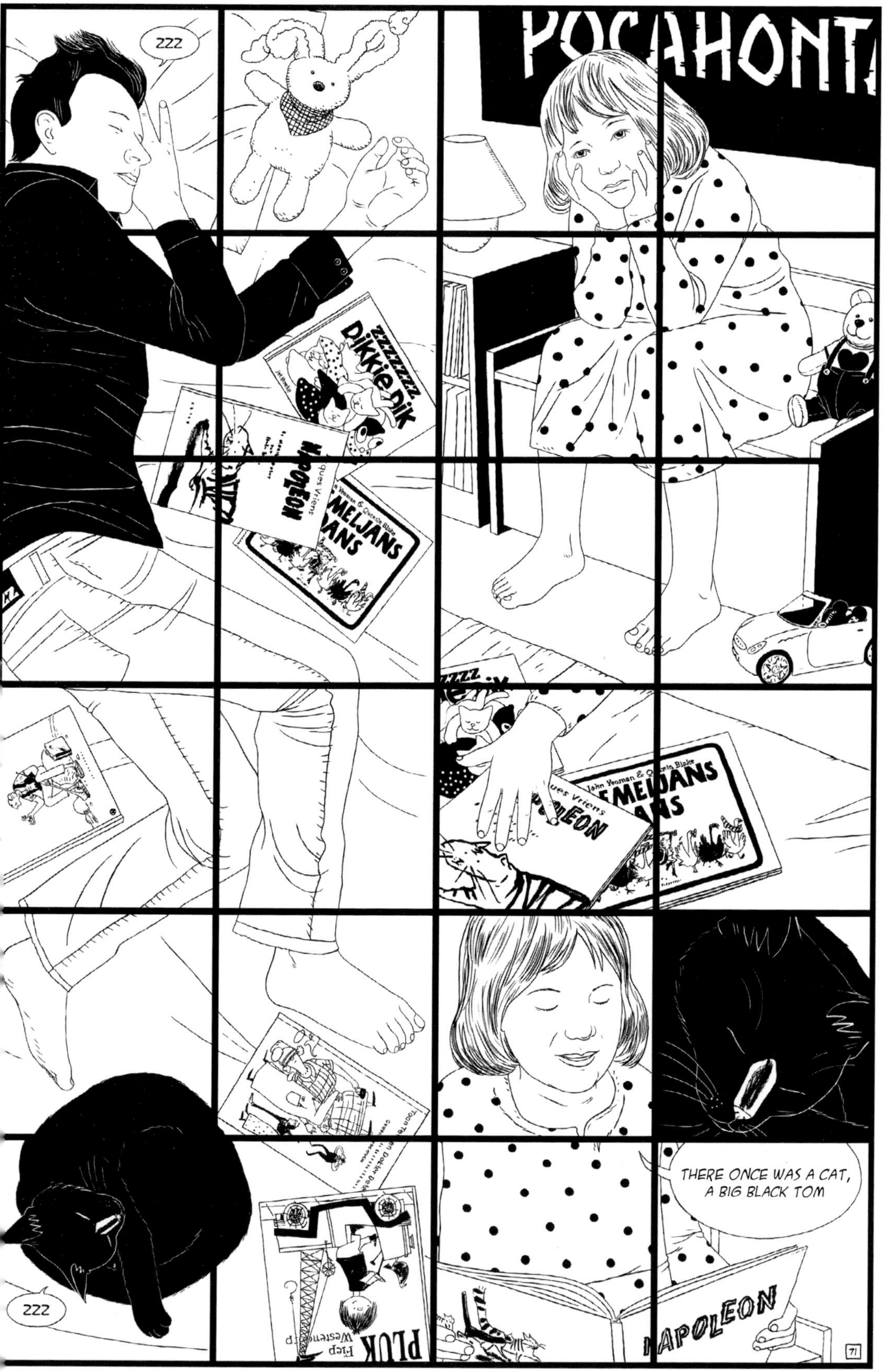
ZZZ
POCAHONTA
Dikkie Dik
NAPOLEON
John Yeoman & Quentin Blake
ZZZ
THERE ONCE WAS A CAT,
A BIG BLACK TOM
NAPOLEON
PLUK
Fiep Westendorp

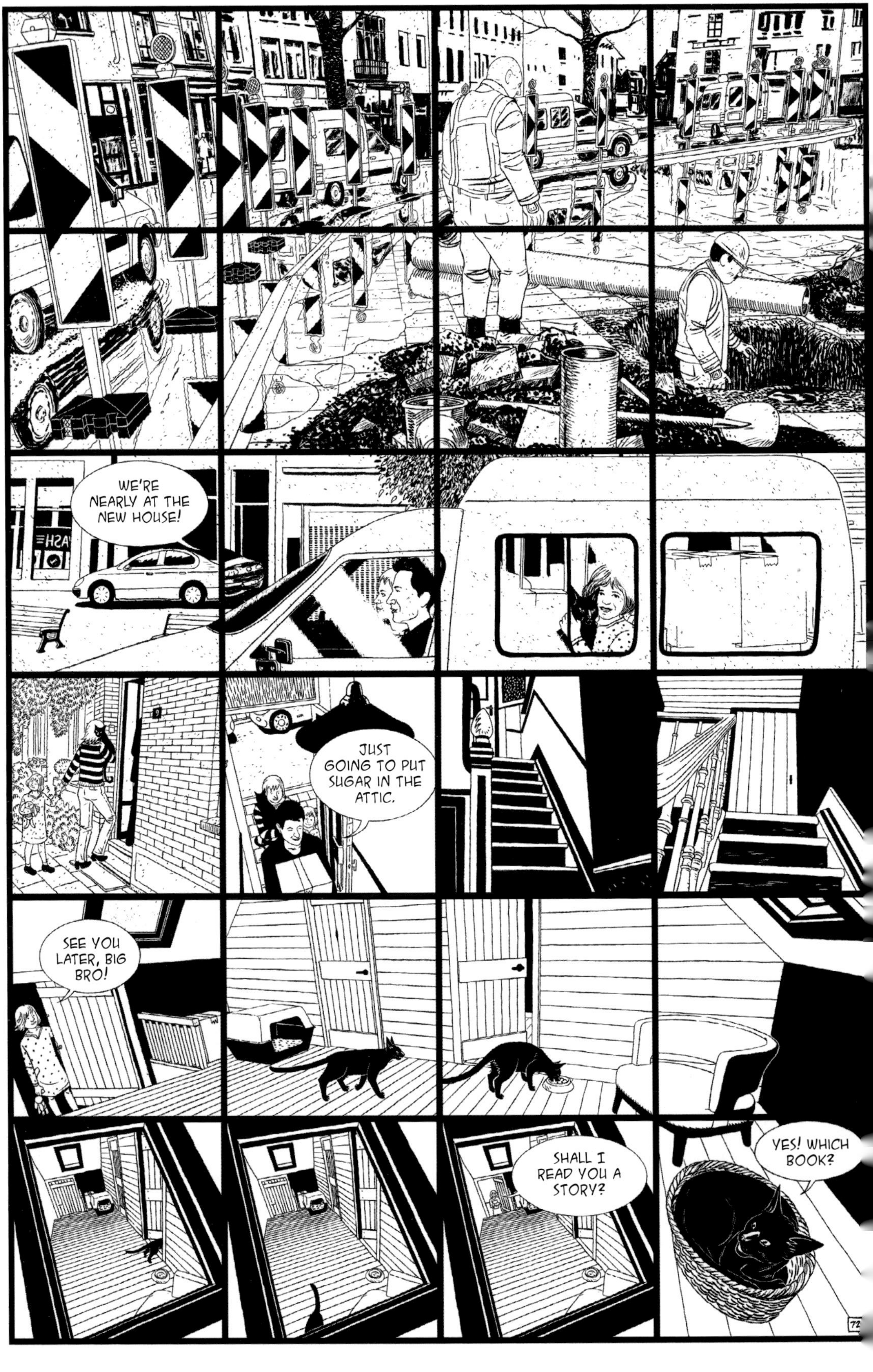
WE'RE NEARLY AT THE NEW HOUSE!
HSA
JUST GOING TO PUT SUGAR IN THE ATTIC.
SEE YOU LATER, BIG BRO!
SHALL I READ YOU A STORY?
YES! WHICH BOOK?

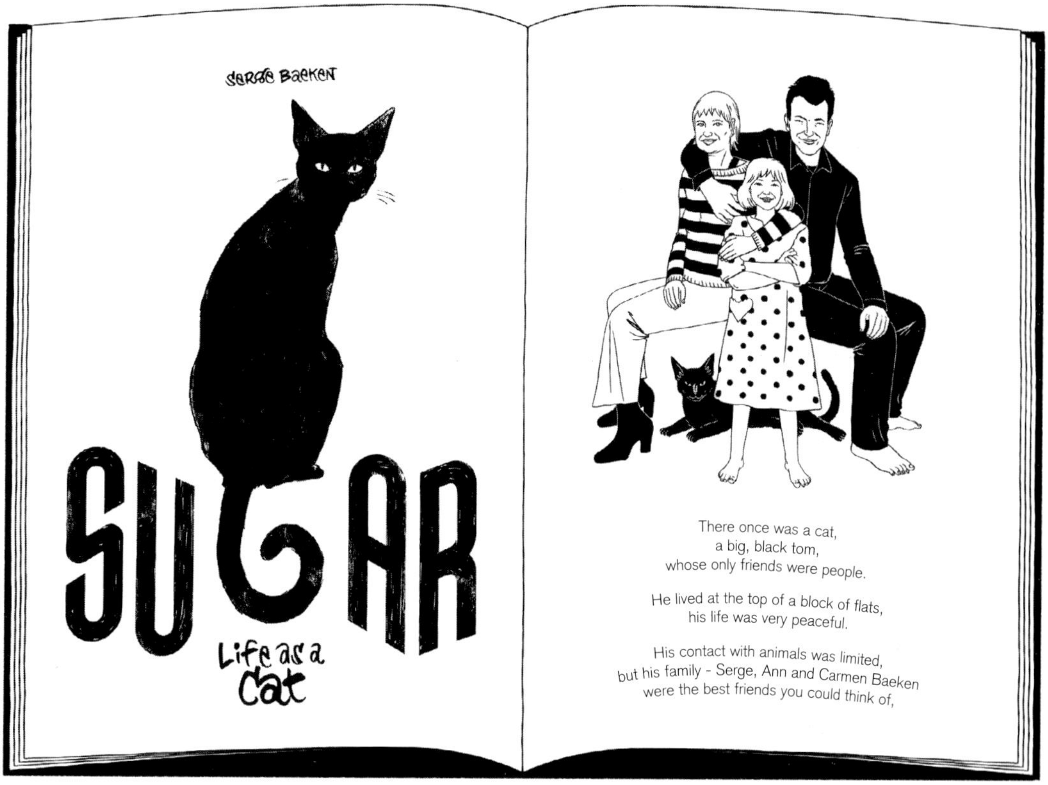
Serge Baeken
SUGAR
Life as a cat
There once was a cat,
a big, black tom,
whose only friends were people.
He lived at the top of a block of flats,
his life was very peaceful.
His contact with animals was limited,
but his family - Serge, Ann and Carmen Baeken
were the best friends you could think of,

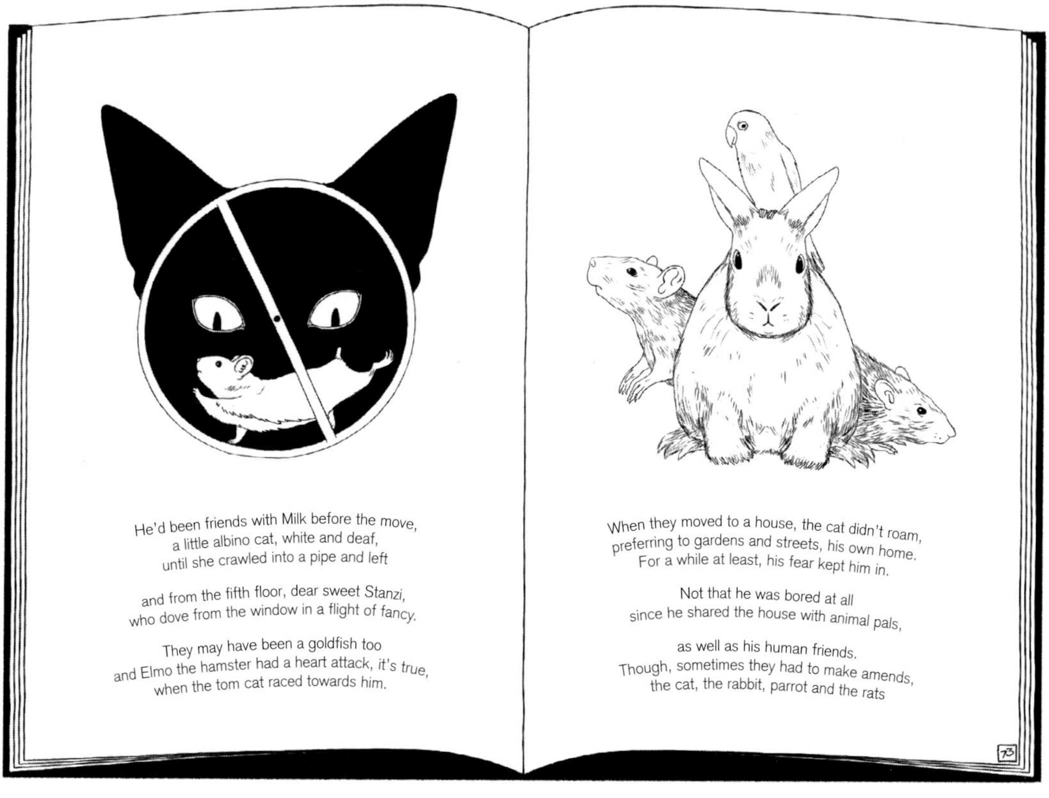
He'd been friends with Milk before the move,
a little albino cat, white and deaf,
until she crawled into a pipe and left
and from the fifth floor, dear sweet Stanzi,
who dove from the window in a flight of fancy.
They may have been a goldfish too
and Elmo the hamster had a heart attack, it's true,
when the tom cat raced towards him.
When they moved to a house, the cat didn't roam,
preferring to gardens and streets, his own home.
For a while at least, his fear kept him in.
Not that he was bored at all
since he shared the house with animal pals,
as well as his human friends.
Though, sometimes they had to make amends,
the cat, the rabbit, parrot and the rats
73

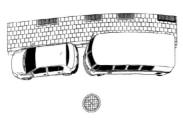

whose names were Ollie, Cookie, Plato and Socrates.
I don't want to say that they hated each other,
but living together is more than just keeping the peace.

When the dead bird was buried, the rabbit rehomed
and Plato and Socrates gone to their maker,

the house was so quiet. Maybe this was the cause
of the tom cat becoming much braver.
He took his first steps in the great outdoors.

At first he'd skulk, then stop stock-still,
skittish and nervous, in the shadow of a wall
or hidden beneath cars parked at the curb

his ears turning into the wind, perturbed
by the slightest unfamiliar sound:

a door closing, a dog yapping,
a laughing neighbour with cane tapping,
a bus setting off, the moon obscured by clouds.

After a while, he stayed out, no longer cowed.
He'd sit at the window when it rained
impatiently waiting for the sun to come out again.

Or he'd sleep with just one eye shut
until it was time to go out and strut

At least he would, if the door were open
Otherwise he'd beg his human friends,
himself being fingerless, to lift the latches again

Light on his feet, elegant and spunky,
the proud king of his minor country
ran through the streets, right down the middle.

This majestic king ruled over the local cat crew
like Solomon, noble, beloved, revered and shrewd.

He listened to the problems of his people
heard their grievances and made things equal
he never missed a nuance in a story or a detail.

He had more friends than I can draw:
Peter, Isis, Tosca, Jules, Captain, Ginger, Cato and Claw
and lots of other cats whose names I forget,

and lots of others whose names I never knew
cats of all shapes and sizes, colours and hues

who lived around here, whom he befriended.
He lived much longer, their lives ended,
but he valued them greatly when they were around.

The tom cat was well known as the toughest in town.
Tail between their legs, opponents were sent packing
But the confrontations were never really nerve-wracking.

After a bit of clawing and hissing and ding-dong,
he'd come in purring to say he'd won

without any serious danger or loss of face.
The days, months, seasons and years raced
The best moments of which we have noted.

Much, much later, he entered his dotage
he became stiffer, greyer, blind and somewhat bald,
He was forced to find his way along the skirting boards.

After eighteen human years or a hundred and twenty-six in cat,
the absolute maximum for felines at that,

Bast wrote a painless ending to his long story.
This merciful God of Cats also heard out his last request:
On the lap of his favourite human to go to his rest,

Deeply saddened and very upset
his human friends used a pram
to transport his lifeless body to the vets

Then they returned to Linden Street
the road in which the tom cat had lived

There was once a cat, a tom cat, an aristocrat
who will enter the whiskery hall of fame,
Sugar was that sweet treasure's name.

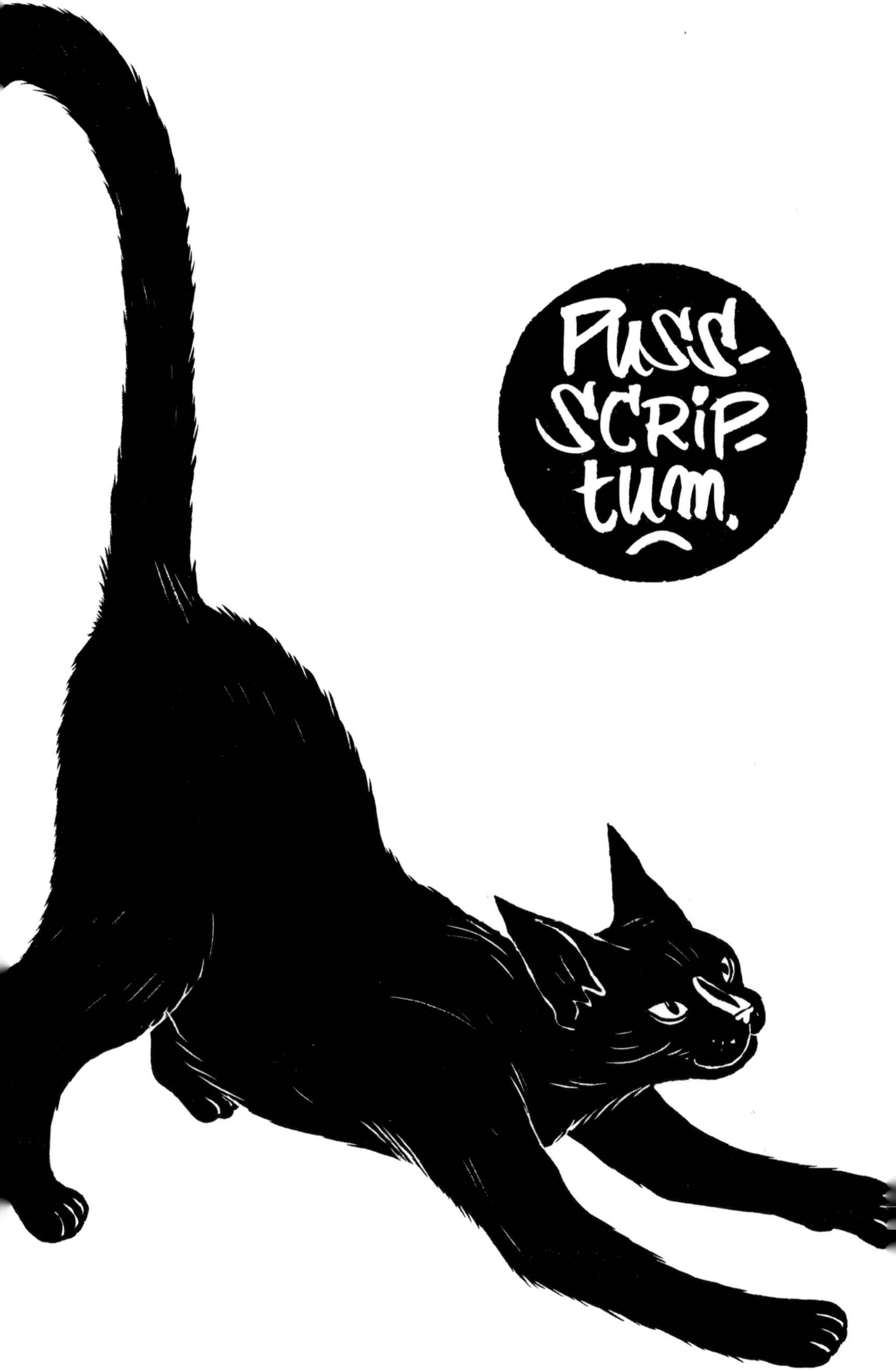
PUSS-
SCRIP-
tum.

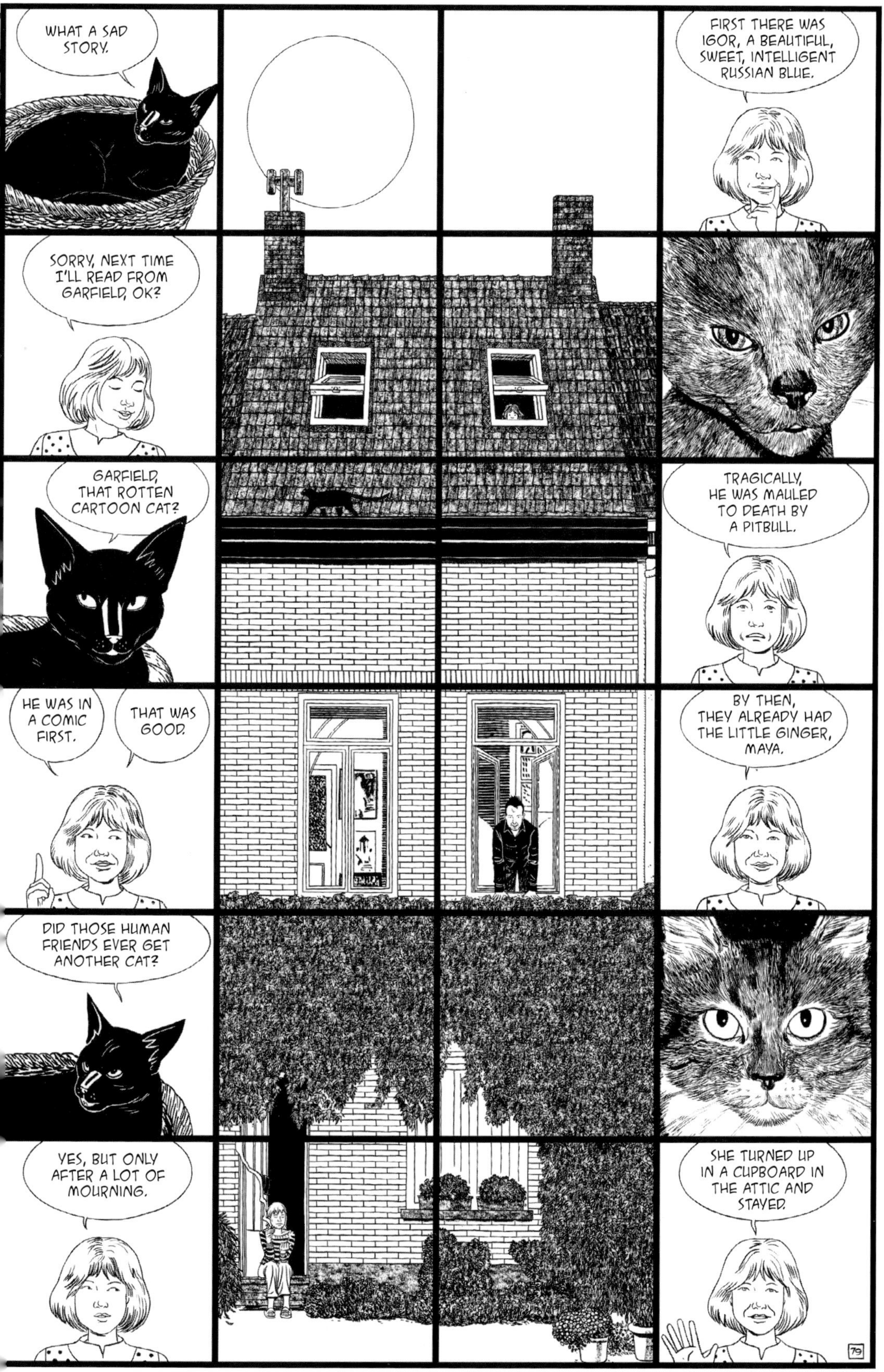
WHAT A SAD STORY.
FIRST THERE WAS IGOR, A BEAUTIFUL, SWEET, INTELLIGENT RUSSIAN BLUE.
SORRY, NEXT TIME I'LL READ FROM GARFIELD, OK?
GARFIELD, THAT ROTTEN CARTOON CAT?
TRAGICALLY, HE WAS MAULED TO DEATH BY A PITBULL.
HE WAS IN A COMIC FIRST.
THAT WAS GOOD.
BY THEN, THEY ALREADY HAD THE LITTLE GINGER, MAYA.
DID THOSE HUMAN FRIENDS EVER GET ANOTHER CAT?
YES, BUT ONLY AFTER A LOT OF MOURNING.
SHE TURNED UP IN A CUPBOARD IN THE ATTIC AND STAYED.
79

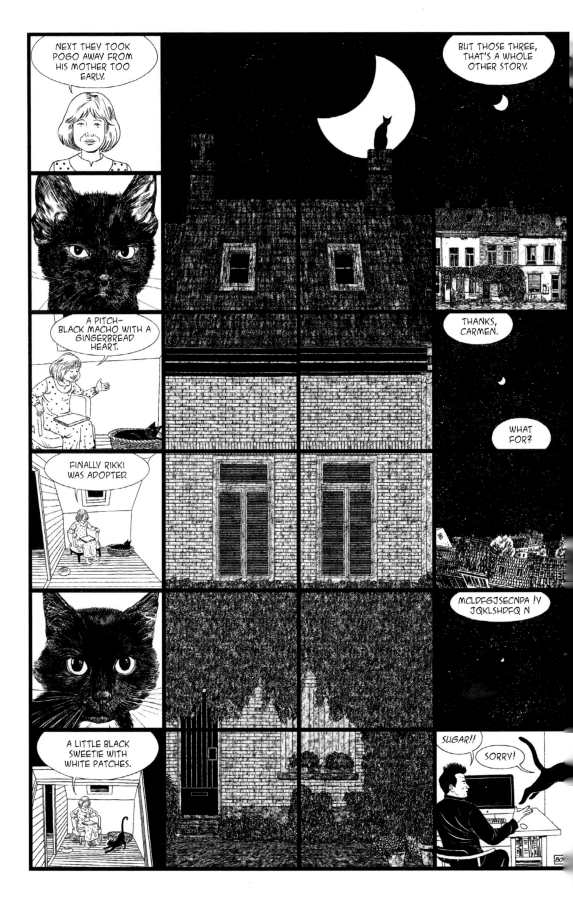

NEXT THEY TOOK POGO AWAY FROM HIS MOTHER TOO EARLY.

BUT THOSE THREE, THAT'S A WHOLE OTHER STORY.

A PITCH-BLACK MACHO WITH A GINGERBREAD HEART.

THANKS, CARMEN.

WHAT FOR?

FINALLY RIKKI WAS ADOPTED.

MCLDFGJSECNPA !Y JQKLSHDFQ N

A LITTLE BLACK SWEETIE WITH WHITE PATCHES.

SUGAR!!

SORRY!

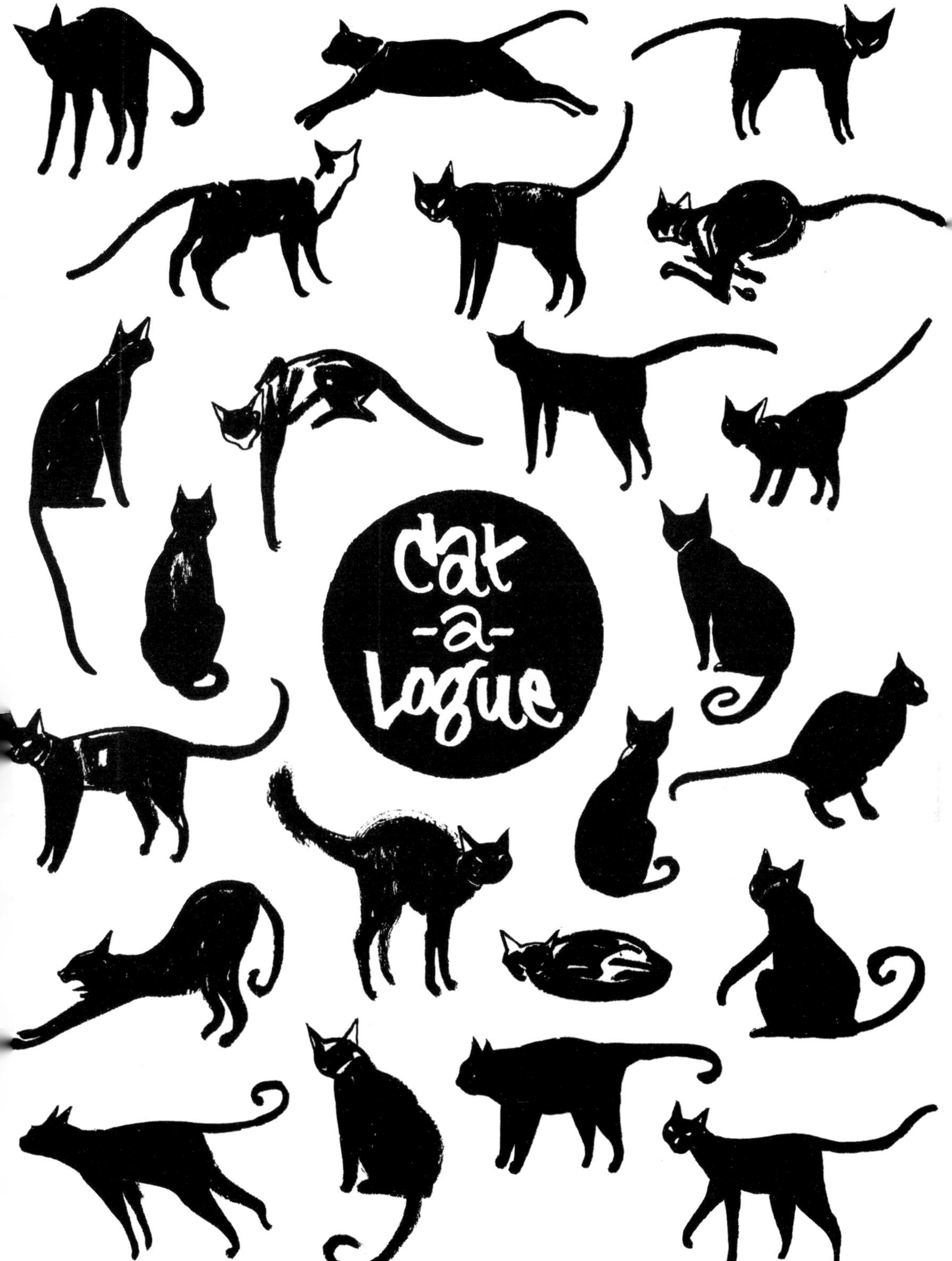
Cat
-a-
Logue

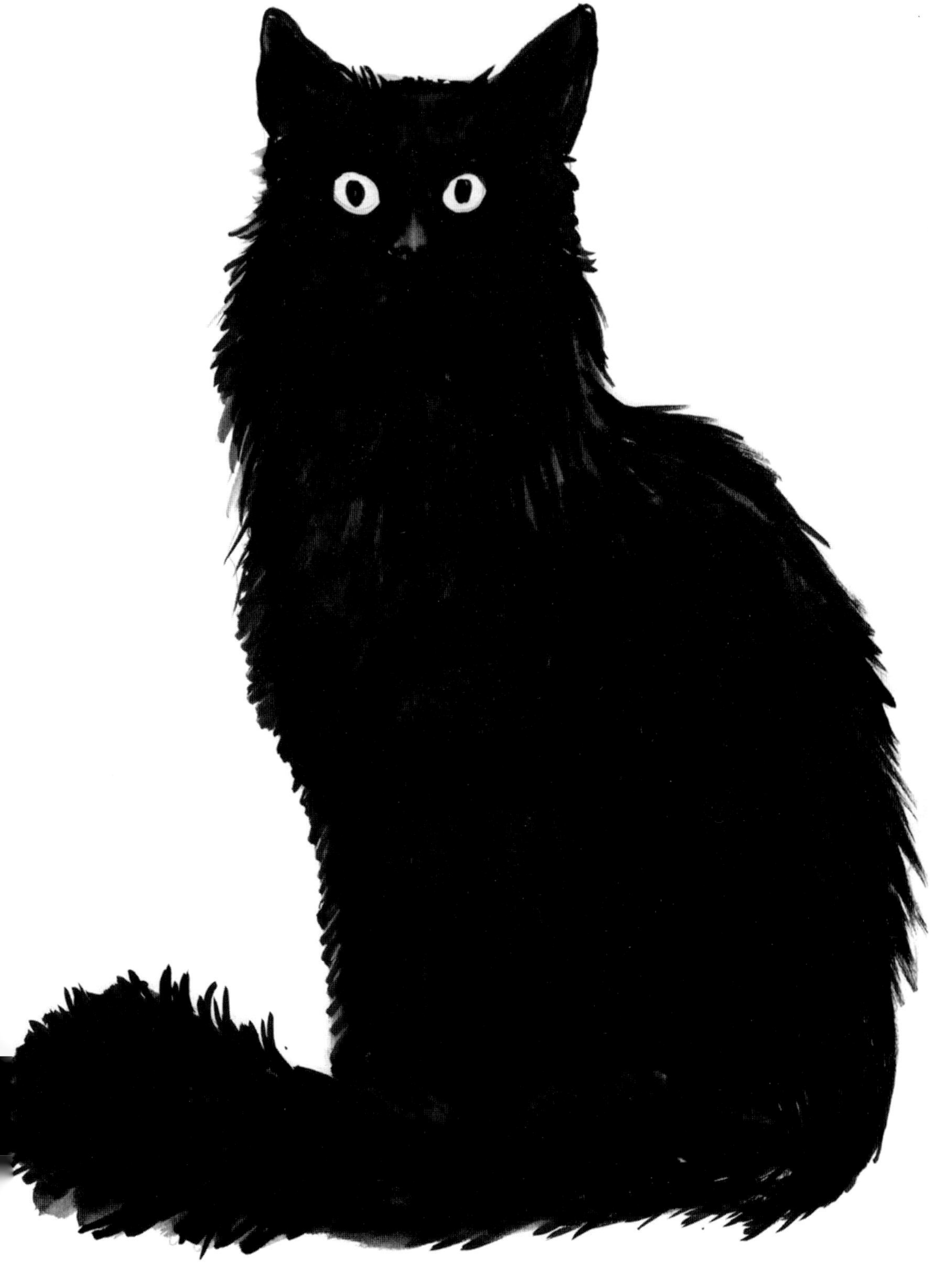

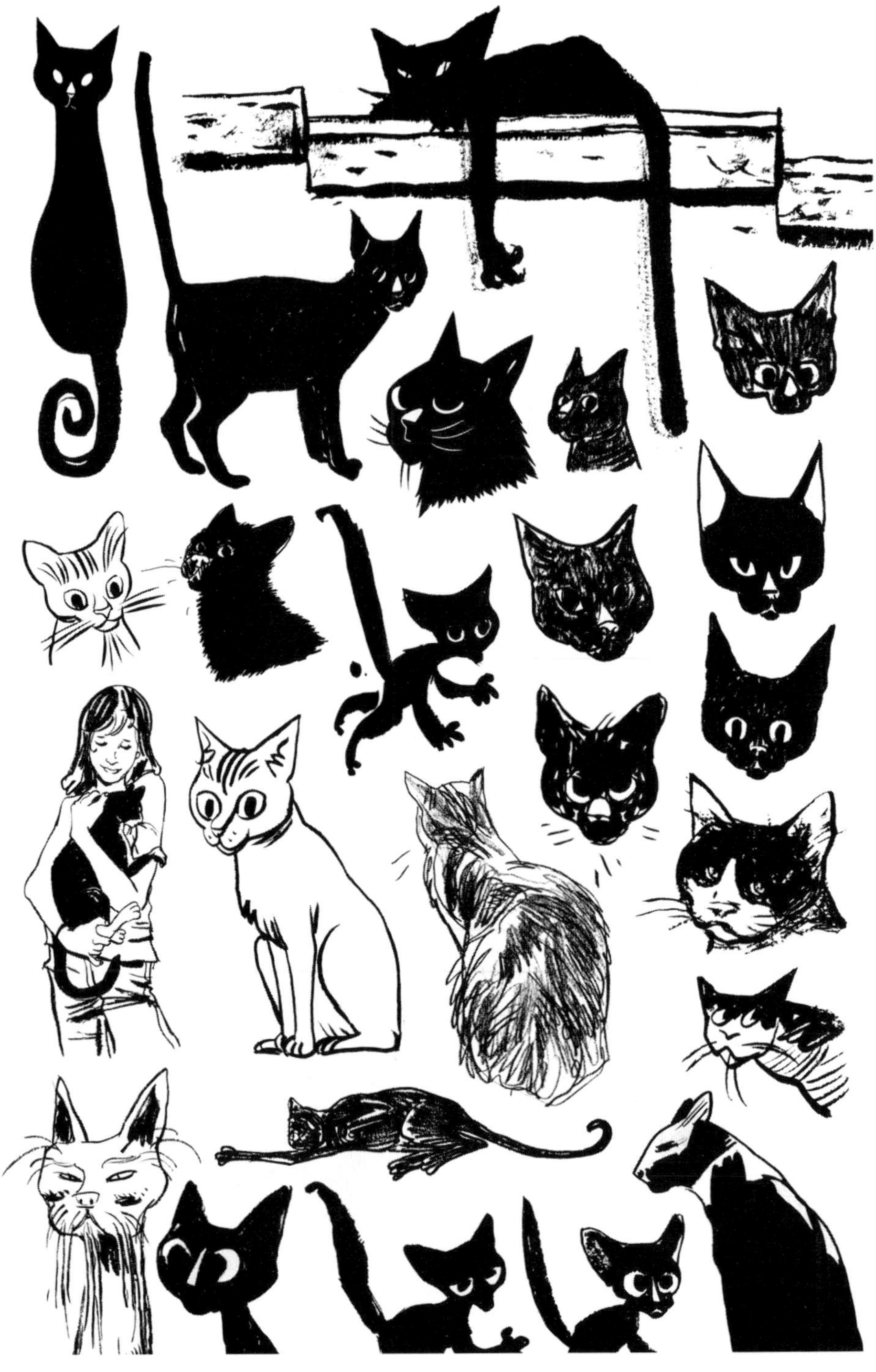

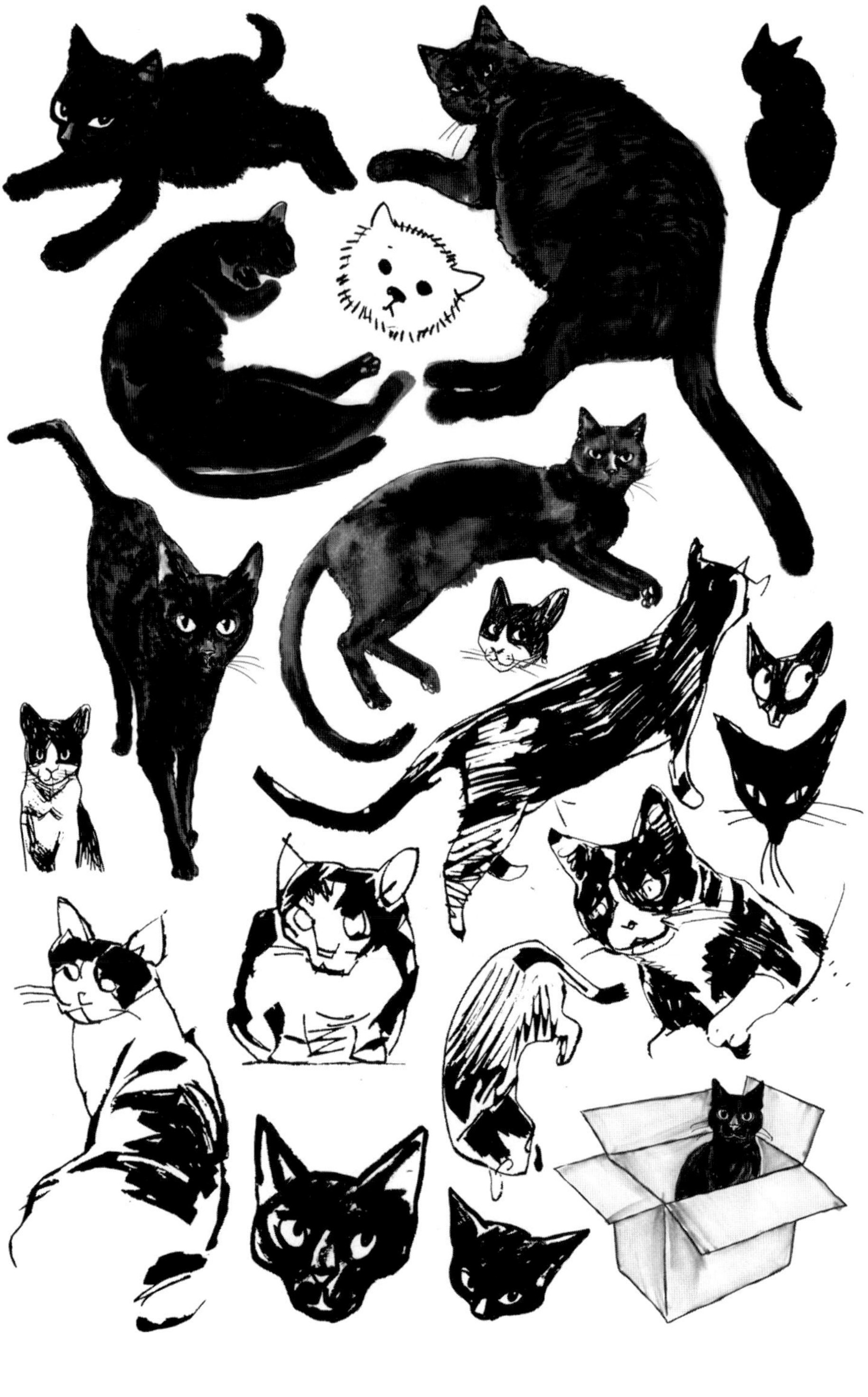

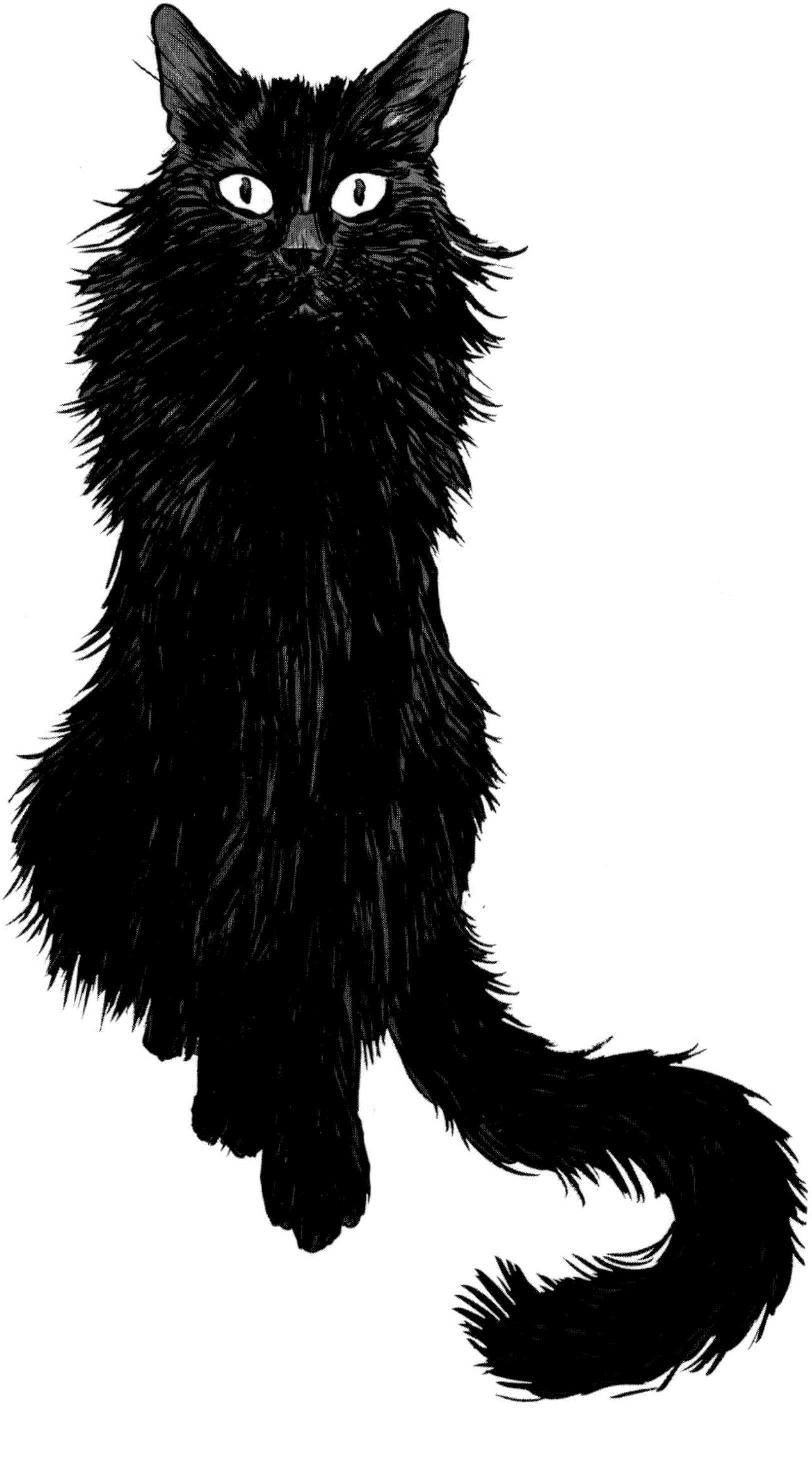

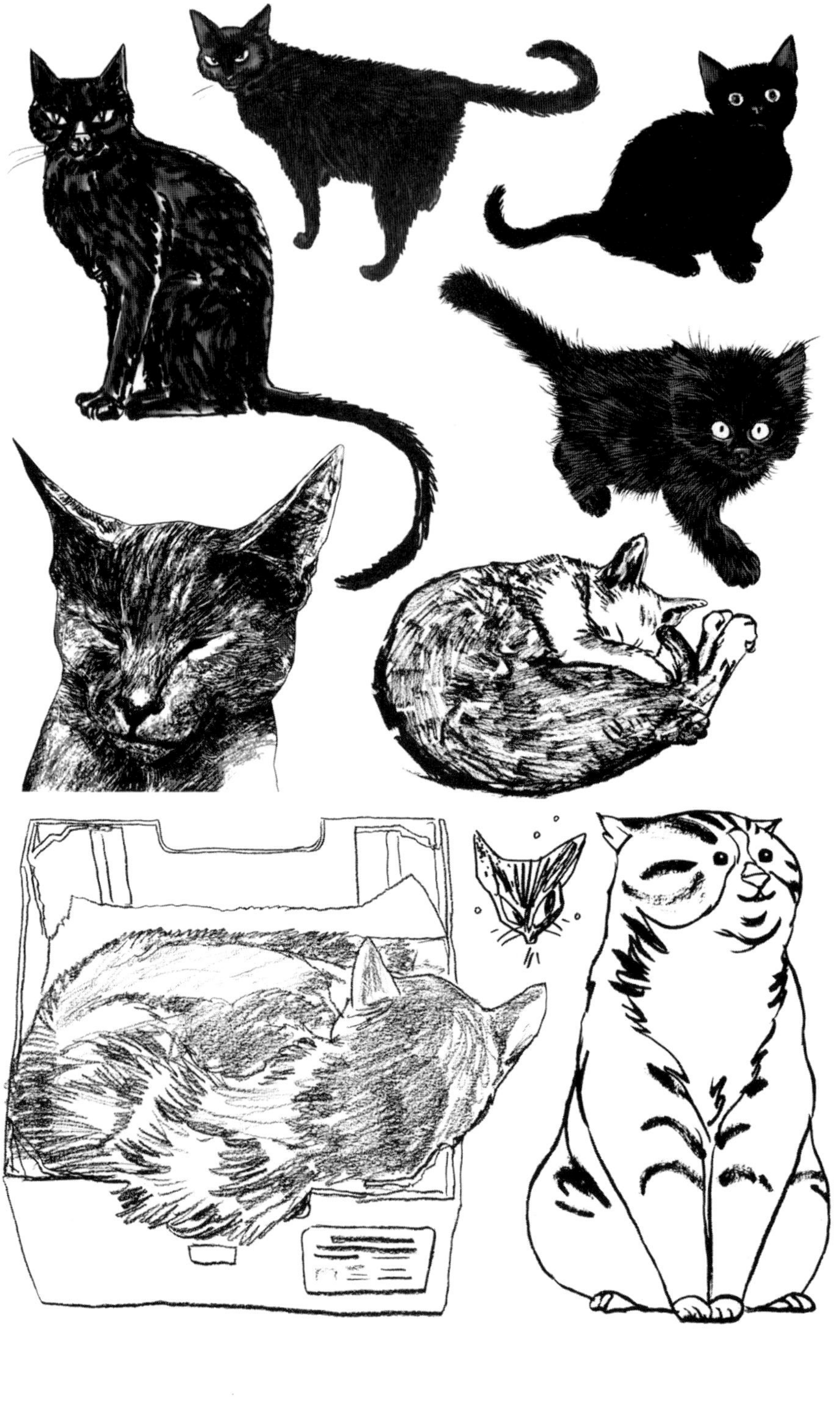

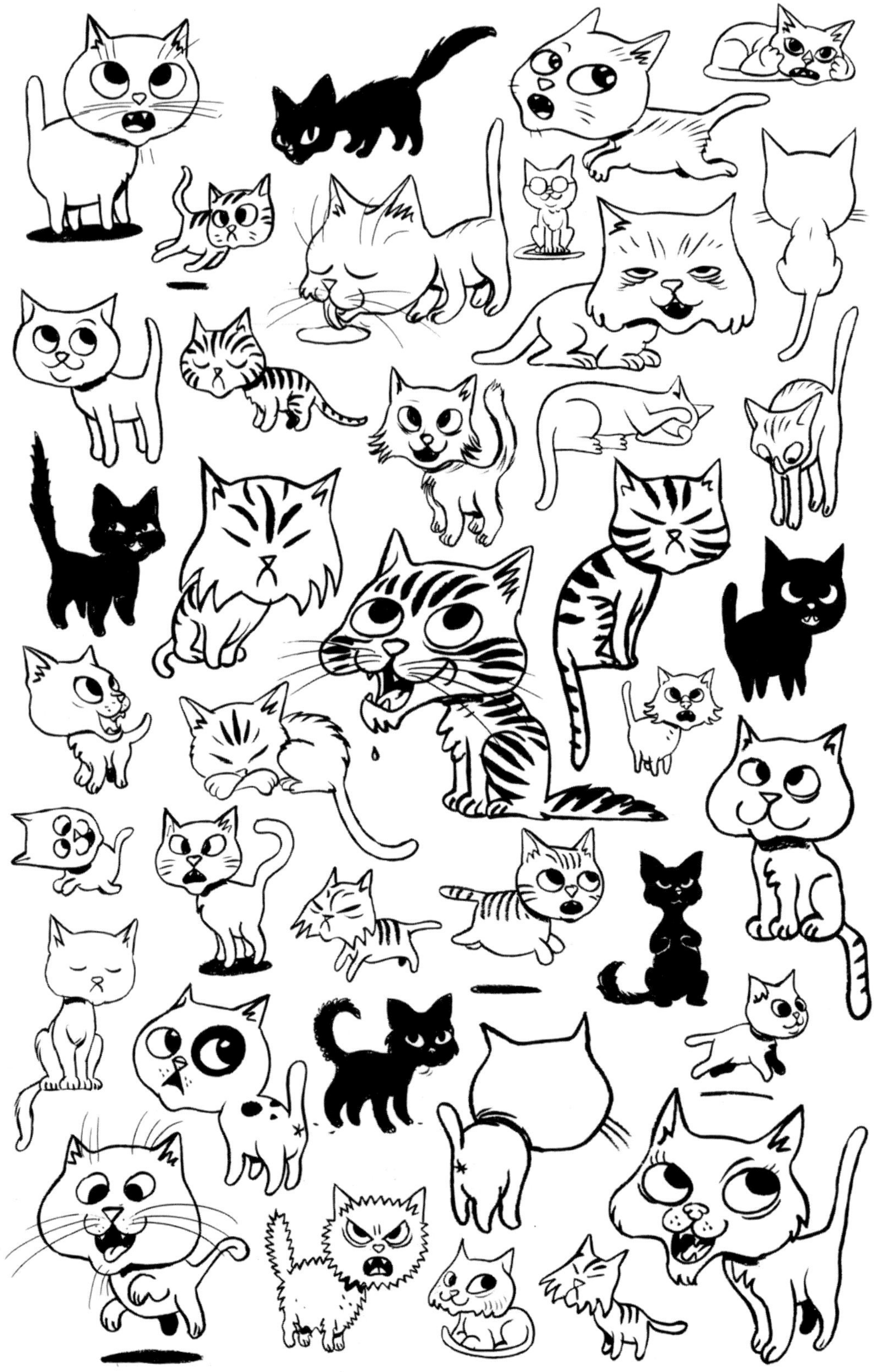

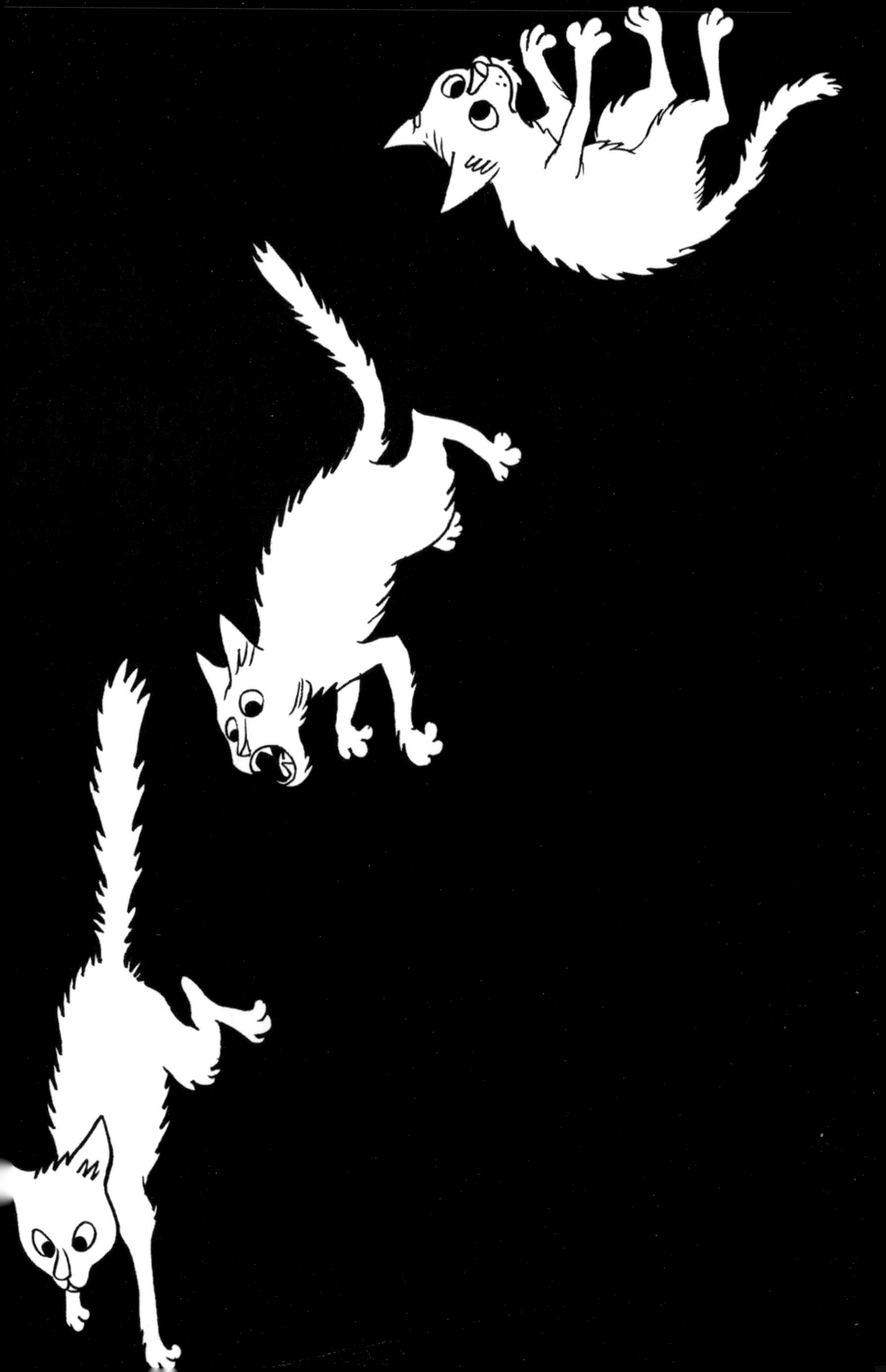

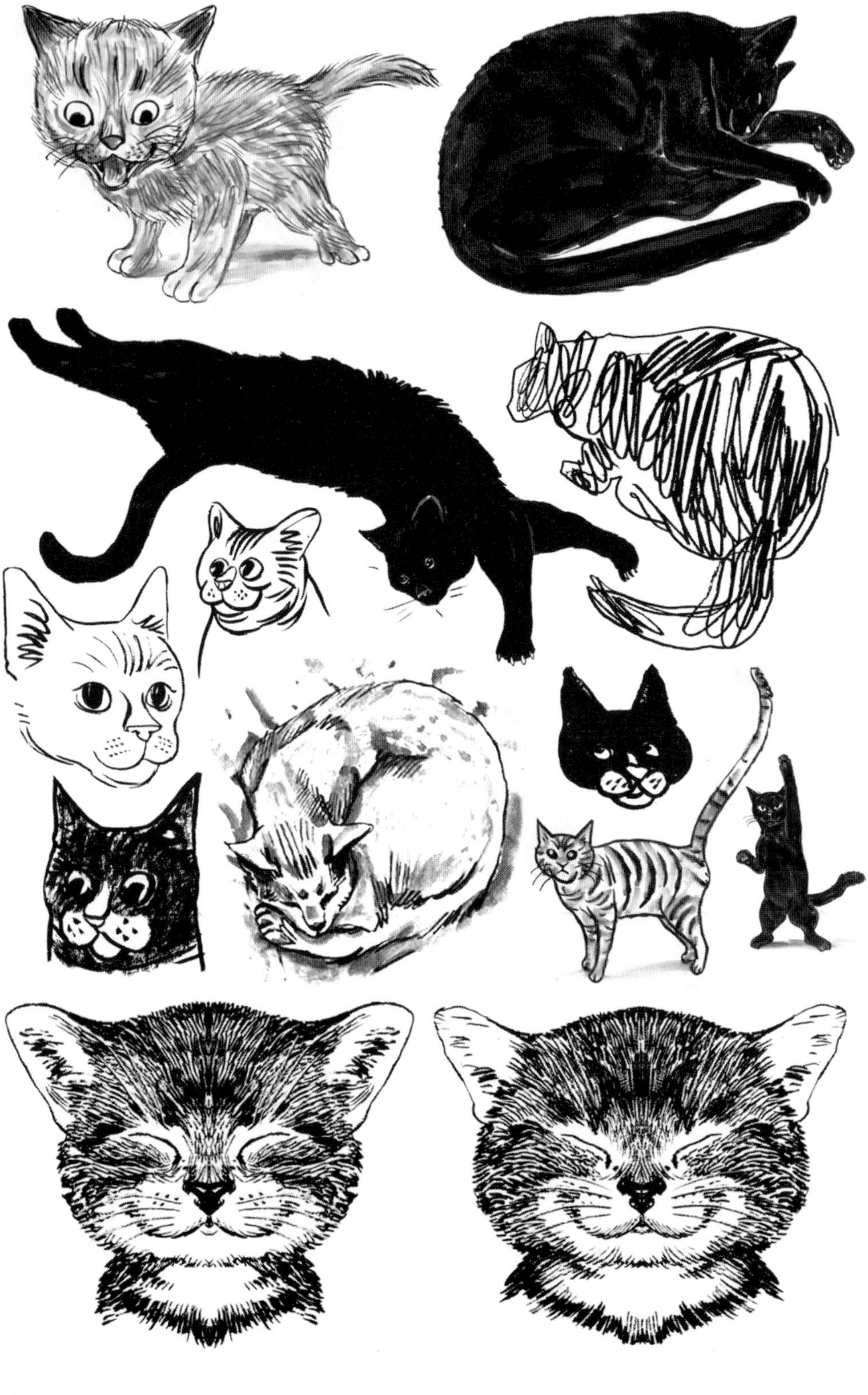

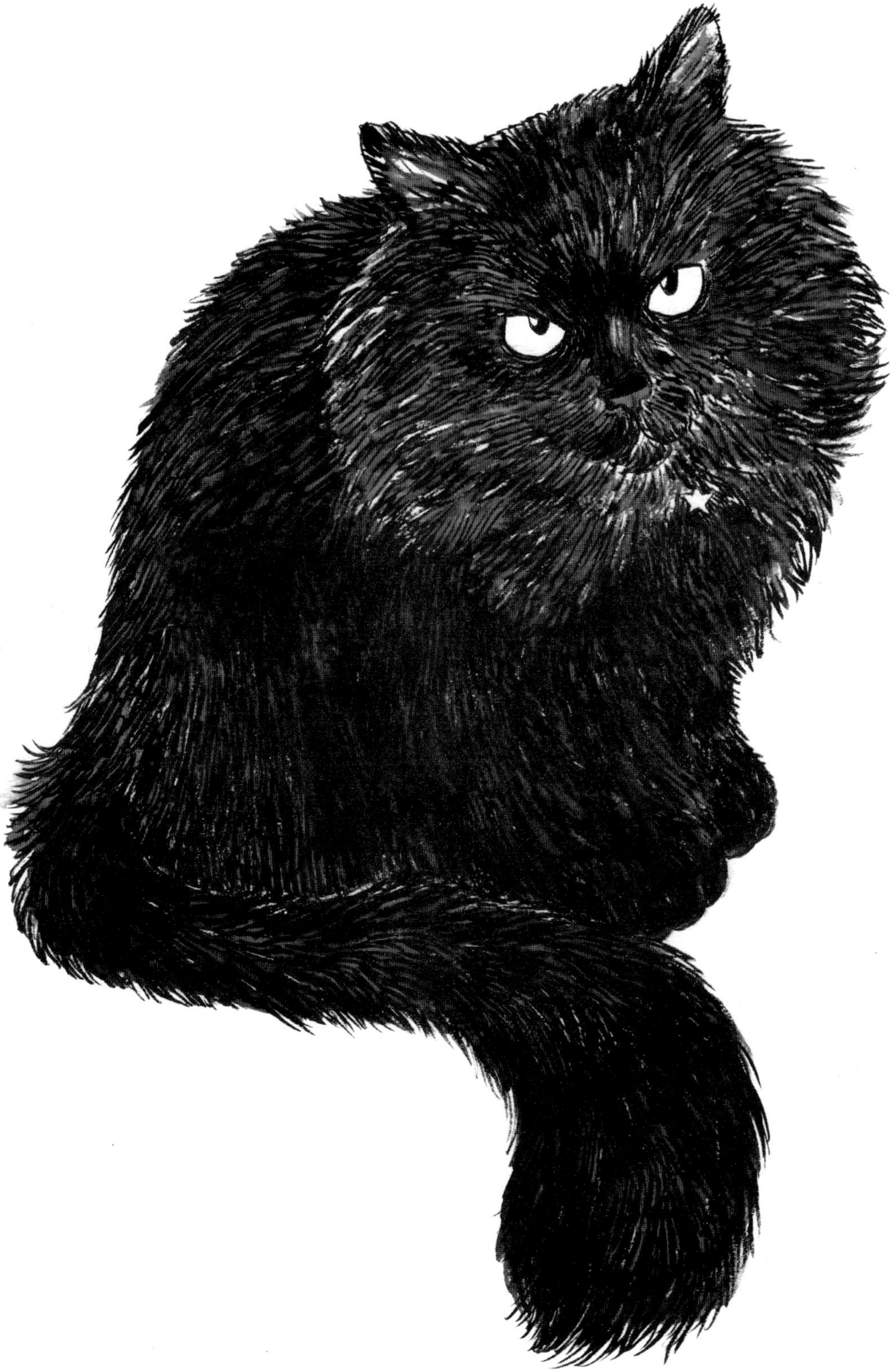

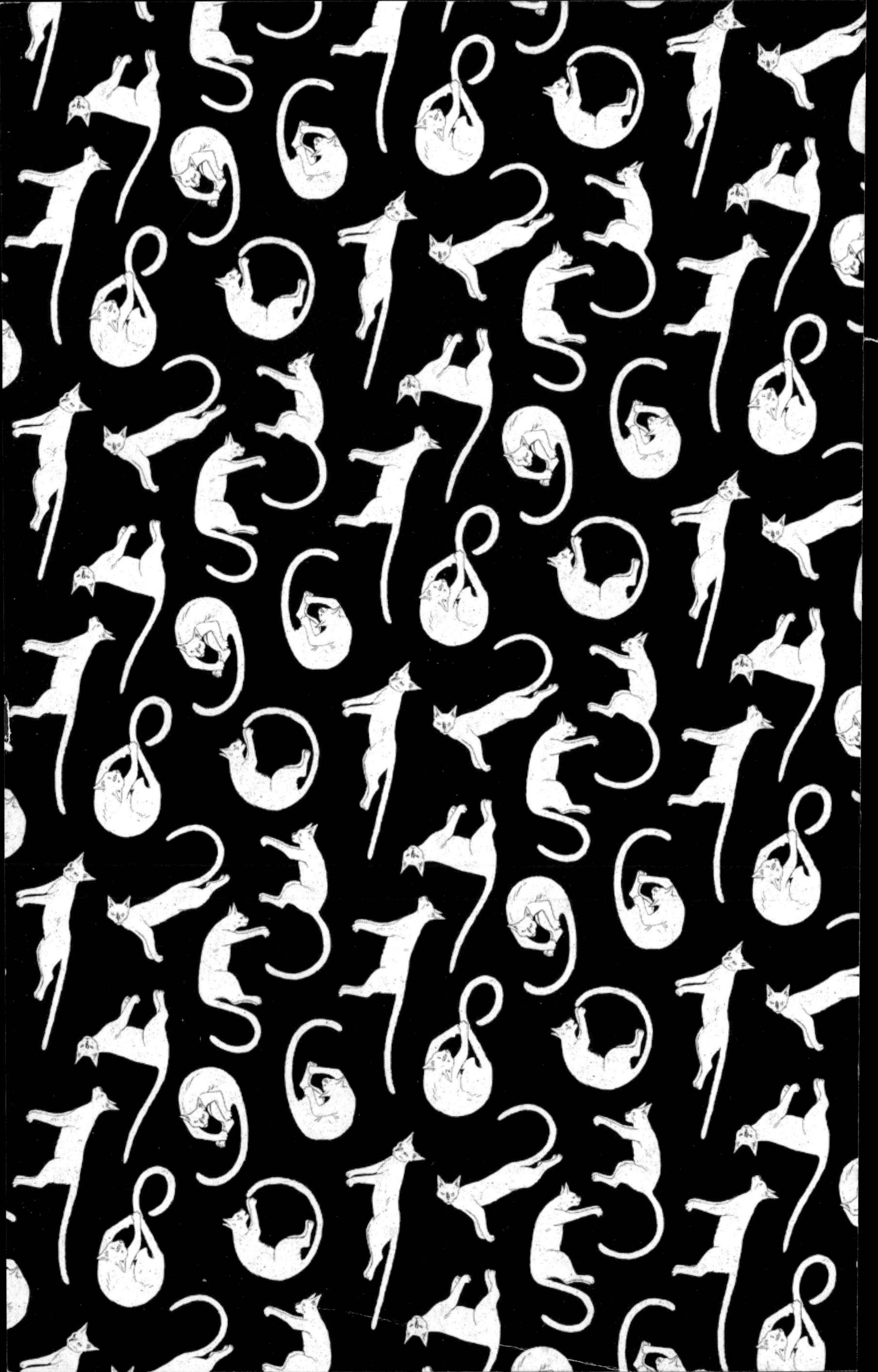